This copy of
'The Boy Who Forgot
to Grow Down'
collected by Tom Baker
belongs to

. . . .

Also available in Sparrow Books:

Never Wear Your Wellies in the House
Poems collected by Tom Baker

THE BOY WHO FORGOT TO GROW DOWN

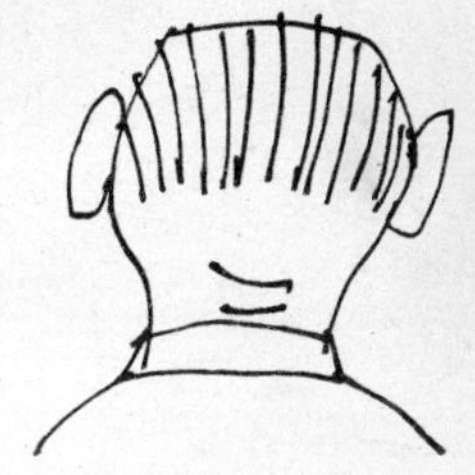

COLLECTED BY

Tom Baker

Illustrated by

Colin West

A Royalty from every copy sold will go to
the charity Help a Child to See

A Sparrow Book
Published by Arrow Books Limited
17–21 Conway Street, London W1P 6JD

An imprint of the Hutchinson Publishing Group

London Melbourne Sydney Auckland
Johannesburg and agencies throughout the world

First published 1984

Set in Linoterm Century Schoolbook
by JH Graphics Limited
Reading, Berks

Made and printed in Great Britain
by the Anchor Press Ltd
Tiptree, Essex

ISBN 0 09 928490 1

Introduction

THE BOY WHO FORGOT TO GROW DOWN. You may well ask what this means. The answer is that it means very little. It's just a bit of nonsense taken from one of the limericks in this collection but it reminds me of all those times we are told to GROW UP. There we are having a great time, when someone invariably says 'Oh, I do wish you'd grow up!' Well, growing up is all very well but sometimes we should forget all about being serious and sensible and settle down to a really good belly laugh. That's where these limericks come in.

This book is published to help a child to see and I would likc to thank the contributors and Caroline Sheldon for such a lot of help. I would also like to thank those of you who buy the book. In return for buying it you should get a bit of a snigger and a funny bone jolt too. So, just for a while, sit back and enjoy a really excellent bit of fun and nonsense.

Never mind what the title means!

Tom Baker

The boy who forgot to grow down
Grew up on the far side of town;
By the time he was seven
He was six-foot-eleven
A figure of highest renown.

Tom Baker

I was talking with Mrs Mal'prop
Who was grabbing a bus at a stop.
Her ears had been 'skewered'
And her nails just 'manured',
She said, at the city's 'Top Shop'.

Alvin Stardust

A hippo who lived in Polgigga
Had a tummy that slowly grew bigger.
They thought that she maybe
Was having a baby,
Which explained such a change in her figure.

Val Hudson and friends

There was a young fellow called Fred,
Whose feet grew out of his head.
He would take off his hat,
Wipe his feet on the mat,
And hop on his nose up to bed.

Sir Harry Secombe

There was a young man called Papp
Who liked a mid-afternoon nap.
One day in Ongar
He slept a lot longer,
And woke up a much older chap.

Michael Palin

Let us all shed a tear for Bob Cratchit
Who was chopping up logs with a hatchet,
When much to his woe
He sliced off a toe,
And he can't find another to match it.

Bob Monkhouse

Did you hear of Mick from County Clare
Who went off skating just for a dare.
On the ice took one pace,
Fell flat on his face,
And said: 'Begorra! It's slippery out there.'

Robin Cousins

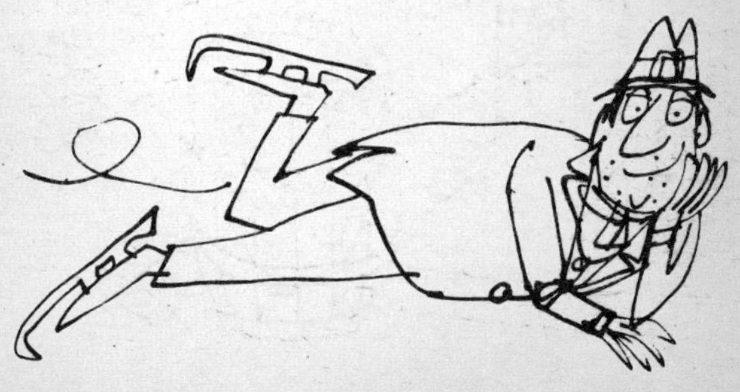

A man called Mad Dan McGrew
Was boiling a cauldron of stew.
For no reason at all
He dived in, clothes and all.
Now if he can – why then can't you?

Spike Milligan

Unfortunate Barrington Pruett
Had a nose that resembled a cruet.
Just to make matters worse
And to add to the curse,
He got covered in salt when he blew it.

Sir Harry Secombe

A man who was driving a jeep
Was trapped by a vast flock of sheep.
He beeped with his horn
Which they treated with scorn
Because sheep go 'Baa, Baa' not 'Beep, Beep'.

Spike Milligan

A footballer with a sore toe
Reported to the physio.
When the team saw his strapping
They all began clapping
'Cos he'd finished it off with a bow.

Arsenal Football Club

A naughty young sailor from Strood
Conceived of a plan rather rude.
He trapped Mary Whitehouse
Inside an old lighthouse
And forced her to dance in the nude.

A and D Newlands

If there's one thing I can't bear, it's writing.
It isn't the least bit exciting.
But you couldn't have guessed,
When you sent your request,
That the whole of my day you'd be blighting.

Victoria Wood

A hill-walker entering Flodden,
Whose feet were uncomfortably sodden,
Was offered a fire
And a Hoover spin-dryer –
A welcome both ancient and modern.

A and D Newlands

There was an MP in the house
Who was always as quiet as a mouse.
But his wife never stopped,
She would talk till he dropped –
So he was replaced by his spouse.

Jack Ashley MP

An affected old Party of Gwent
Said, 'I fear I can never assent
To the sort of bow-ties
Which revolve. Who denies
They're the mark of the cad, not the gent?'

But a flâneur from near Ballylickey
Tartly asked: 'Isn't that rather picky?
I find I deplore
One who lays down the law
When he's wearing a celluloid dickey.'

Robert Robinson

A child called Alice M'Forethought
Dropped a stink bomb in somebody's forecourt.
Though she knew it was wrong
To make such a pong,
She did it with malice aforethought.

Jean Ure

There once was an ancient Peruvian,
Whose manners were antediluvian.
After bolting his food,
He was often so rude
As to belch in a manner Vesuvian.

Richard Heller

There was a young girl called Ann
Who fried her goldfish in a pan.
Adding salt and then pepper
Didn't make it taste better –
And then she was sick over gran.

Simon Cann, Age 11, Moseley Junior School

A man from the Mull of Kintyre
Said, 'My bagpipes are always for hire.'
When he started to play
He was shot at, they say,
Which deflated them just like a tyre.

Spike Milligan

There was a young man of Bury
Who couldn't write words that rhymed.
When he got to the end
Of a line, he wrote things
That didn't fit – most of the time anyway.

Mike Harding

There was a young student from Chatham
Who hated exams when he sat 'em.
The papers, he said,
Gave him pains in the head,
With their muddled inadequate datum.

A and D Newlands

There was a young lad called Gary
Who always wanted to marry,
When he got to the church
He was left in the lurch –
Oh, the poor young lad called Gary.

Samantha Clugston, Age 13, John Aird School

There was a young fellow named Sam
Who loved tucking into the jam;
When his mother said, 'Sammy,
Don't make yourself jammy.'
He said, 'You're too late, Ma, I am!'

Langford Reed

There was a young girl from Prestatyn
Who made herself knickers of satin.
For her classical friends
To peruse as she bends,
She embroidered the edges in Latin.

David Hatch

An earnest young lady called Botts
Could tie most incredible knots –
Double granny or reef
With a hitch underneath –
But none of them cleared up her spots.

Michael Palin

A newscaster from Argentina
Committed a grave misdemeanour:
In a radio talk
He spoke of the Falk-
lands, though his people call them 'Malvina'.

Denis Healey MP

There was a young man called Dennis
Who on the golf course was often a menace.
But when out in the field,
His bat he would wield –
Perhaps he should take up tennis.

Dennis Amiss

An agent from far Uruguay
Was the world's most incompetent spy.
He hid for ten days
In Hampton Court maze
Because he was frightened to die.

Richard Heller

A facetious young bowler from Stoke
Bowled a hand grenade once for a joke.
But he ran out of luck
When the firing pin stuck,
Leaving only black flannels and smoke.

Ian Botham

A stoker who comes from Kitzbühl
Was warned as he worked like a mule:
'If you're careless, your toe'll
Get covered in coal,
And you'll then look a bit of a fuel.'

Philip Gross

There was an old man from Harrow
Who sold fresh veg from a barrow.
During the night
He got in a fight,
And had his head stuffed in a marrow.

Maria Worboys, Age 17, Park Dean School

The vicar of Pevensey Bay
Went abroad for a year and a day.
His flock, off the tether,
Assembled together,
And took a decision to stray.

A and D Newlands

An archbishop, to keep himself calm,
Kept pigs on a Hertfordshire farm;
The grunts and the snores
Of the prize-winning boars
To Episcopal ears were as balm!

Robert Runcie, Archbishop of Canterbury

A family who comes from Cropedy
Are noted for being quite weedy:
There is one young niece
Who is grossly obese –
But she, I'm afraid, is just greedy.

David Hatch

A dieting damsel from Spittal,
Who frantically wanted to whittle
Away some more fat,
Disappeared – just like that!
Not a jot's left, or even a tittle.

A and D Newlands

Here's a wonderful method I've found
To help you all clean up your town;
Please let me explain,
All you need do is train
All your pigeons to fly upside down.

Johnny Ball

There was a young man called Strathspey
Who swallowed a pigeon one day.
He felt such a twerp,
He made himself burp
And the pigeon flew out and away.

Michael Palin

There was a young man from Rangoon
Who was sent high up in a balloon.
He saw all the stars
From Venus to Mars,
And waved to the Man in the Moon.

Colin Batchelor, Age 18, Park Dean School

There was a young man of Rangoon –
I'm sure that he came from Rangoon.
It wasn't Calcutta,
That's right – not Calcutta,
Yes, I'm sure that he came from Rangoon.

Spike Milligan

In a ladies' boutique known as Anna's
A fruiterer boomed with no manners:
''Ere gimme a scarf!'
But Anna said (with a laugh),
'Yes, sir, we have no bandanas.'

Philip Gross

There is a young lady from Wales
Who wants to play cricket with males.
She'd like to be queen
Of this masculine scene,
And she keeps trying hard, but she fails.

David Hatch

A flea and a fly in a flue
Were imprisoned so what could they do?
Said the fly, 'Let us flee.'
Said the flea,'Let us fly.'
So they flew through a flaw in the flue.

Traditional

There once was a man from St Bees
Who got horribly stung by a wasp.
When asked, 'Does it hurt?'
He said, 'Not at all:
I'm glad it wasn't a hornet.'

W. S. Gilbert

There once was a man called Dick Turpin
Who got an attack of the burpin'.
To Black Bess's horror,
He was up till the morrow,
Right up till the birds started chirpin'.

Geoff Capes

There was a young flautist from Bala
Who entertained men in the parlour.
But the things that she played
Not infrequently strayed
Quite a long way from Mozart and Mahler.

David Hatch

There was a young man from Dragoon
Who thought he could play a good tune.
When asked to play
He said, 'No, not today.
My fiddle is in the lagoon.'

Brian Wright, Age 16, Park Dean School

A milking machine is a boon
To a farmer who keeps it in tune.
But forget how to work it,
The thing will short circuit
And the cow will jump over the moon.

Philip Gross

There was a young man who said, 'Cheese
Is best made by using the knees.
You can make Cheshire
Without too much pressure,
But Cheddar's a bit of a squeeze.'

Peter Buckley Hill

A policeman on duty in Bow
Saw the traffic piled up in a row.
With the traffic lights dead
He just stood on his head
Shouting, 'On yer marks, ready, set, go!'

Spike Milligan

A vegetarian vicar of Bray
Climbed into his pulpit one day.
And thinking of food,
(And not God as he should),
Said to his flock: 'Lettuce pray. . . .'

Leonard Gregory

There once was a cleric bemused
And totally bothered by cruise.
Said he on his knees:
'Dear God, if you please,
Let me have the strength to refuse.'

Monsignor Bruce Kent

There once was a young boy called Neil
Who insisted on eating some peel.
He ate, oh so much!
That he soon could not touch
His toes or the back of his heel.

Moses Cain, Age 11, Moseley Junior School

There was a young girl from Surrey
Who burnt her mouth with hot curry.
She got in a state
And bashed down the gate,
And then ran down the road in a flurry.

Emma Twyman, Age 11, Blatchington Court School

There was a magician from Harlech
Who turned himself into a dalek.
He could function for weeks
If you fed him on leeks
And occasional spoonfuls of garlic.

David Hatch

An ill-fated lady from Thanet,
Who looked rather like a wild gannet,
Grown tired with folk staring,
Announced with great daring:
'I'm off to a far distant planet.'

A and D Newlands

There was this little boy called Syd
Who was a little bit shy as a kid.
But he grew up to be
A heart-throb, believe me,
'Cos little Syd is Syd Little, no kid.

Eddie Large

Baby Eddie was always in charge –
He could even tell butter from marge.
But he kept eating stew,
And he just grew and grew,
And that's why Baby Eddie is Large.

Syd Little

There was an old lady called Nelly
Whose hobby was watching the telly.
She sat there one night
And shivered with fright,
So now she's turned out like a jelly.

Helen Rainone, Age 12, Blatchington Court School

My auntie was awfully demure,
And her mind was so frightfully pure,
That she fainted away
At a friend's house one day
When she saw some canary manure.

Bob Monkhouse

There was a young lady from Leeds
Who wanted some cash for her needs.
She proposed to a baker
Who did not forsake her –
Now she's got all the dough that she kneads.

Bob Monkhouse

There once was a young lady called Valerie
Who got heavy from too many calories.
She gave up her sweets
Her chocolates, her treats
So now Valerie's lost those odd calories.

Joanne McAllister, Age 10, Moseley Junior School

A footballer with just one bootlace
Was sent from the field in disgrace.
He was just going to shoot
When he lost his left boot –
And it struck Jimmy Hill in the face!

Keith Birkinshaw, Tottenham Hotspur FC

There was an old man in a kilt,
When the ferris wheel started to tilt,
Cried: 'Alas, what's concealed
Will too soon be revealed!
It's the beastliest wheel ever built!'

Gavin Ewart

There once was a lady of Rhyll
Who seemed to have babies at will.
When she'd had twenty-eight,
She announced (rather late),
'I think I shall go on the pill.'

David Hatch

A stuttering fellow from Barry
Had made up his mind to m-marry.
His chosen young mate
Said, 'You'll just have to wait!'
He replied, 'I can't t-t-t-tarry.'

A and D Newlands

A camel who had two humps
Thought he had got the mumps.
A doctor called Murray
Said, 'Camel, don't worry,
They're not mumps, they're two lumps caused by
    thumps.'

Spike Milligan

A tough little tadpole called Trevor
Once thought he was terribly clever.
From his pool he uncurled
To discover the world. . . .
Now he's squashed by ten pounds of shoe leather.

Linda Hoy

There was a young man from Crewe
Who decided to build a canoe.
When on the river
He found with a shiver,
That he hadn't used waterproof glue.

Abner George, Blatchington Court School

As a candidate trying to woo
The public far more than *Who's Who*.
It wasn't quite nice –
They uncovered my vice
Of living in style in a zoo.

Alexander Thynne, Viscount Weymouth

There was a young boy called Robby,
Whose father worked as a bobby.
He arrested his son
For pestering his mum –
That poor young boy called Robby.

Ajmal Sheikh, Age 13, John Aird School

There was a bad youngster of Norway
Who wedged his papa in a doorway.
Such rudeness is rather
Unfair to one's father –
I'm awfully glad it's not your way.

Langford Reed

A reckless young lad from Dunbar
Who drove an extremely fast car,
Was said by his teacher
To be a wild creature,
Who, none could deny, would go far.

A and D Newlands

A violinist who played on the telly
Compounded a curious jelly.
It gave strength to the arms
For the playing of Brahms –
But I'm sorry to say it was smelly!

Norman Hunter

The fun-loving mayor of Porthcawl
Was planning a huge civic ball.
It was meant for the gentry,
But rockers gained entry:
They've had to rebuild the town hall.

A and D Newlands

There was a young man from Belfast
Who thought he could run very fast.
He fell on his face
At the start of the race,
And instead of first he came last.

Mary Peters

There was a young man called O'Rick
Who really felt ever so sick.
He drank some new plonk,
And then he got dronk,
And all he could say was 'Hick! Hick!'

Robert Sherman, Age 11, Moseley Junior School

There was a young man from Darjeeling
Who got on a bus bound for Ealing.
It said on the door:
'Please don't spit on the floor,'
So he got up and spat on the ceiling.

Traditional

There was a young mountaineer
Who of heights had simply no fear.
So he gave up all working,
(Some said it was shirking)
And climbing is now his career.

Chris Bonington

There was a young man from Dunbarton
Who said he could run like a Spartan.
He ran just one lap
And his braces went *snap*,
And his face went as red as his tartan.

Andy Hing, Moseley Junior School

An arrogant athlete called Paine
Used to boast he could outsprint a train.
But this 'World's Number One'
In the end was outrun
By a tummy bug picked up in Spain.

Mick Gowar

Said my teenager son with a frown
'I'm the only young man in this town
With a skin that's quite bare . . .
No fuzz and no hair . . .
I'm the boy who forgot to grow down!'

Bob Monkhouse

There was a young lady called Sheldon,
Who went out incredibly seldom.
She said it was nerves
And fear of sharp curves –
But those in the know blame Huw Wheldon.

Michael Palin

A train driver living in Crewe
Went down with a bad dose of 'flu.
He snuffled and wheezed
And, of course, when he sneezed
He went: 'AH-CHOO Choo Choo Choo Choo
Choo!'

Jeremy Nicholas

An explorer named Mortimer Craft,
While in Africa ate spiced giraffe.
The effect of this food
Was a sound deep and rude
And green flames that shot out fore and aft.

Mick Gowar

There was a young lady of York
Who found herself armed with a fork.
She ran after a pig
And gave it a dig,
And had a nice mouthful of pork.

Judi Dench

A chappie who came from New York
Tried to teach a parrot to talk.
But what a curse,
It worked in reverse,
Now he goes around going 'Squawk'.

Spike Milligan

There was an old poacher called Bruce
Whose belt was always too loose.
One day in the town
His trousers fell down,
And out came three cats and a goose.

Michael Palin

There was a young fellow from Skye
Who was four feet three inches high.
He wed a ladee
Who was six foot three
With whom he saw eye to thigh.

Robin Hawdon

There was a young woman from Crewe
Who wrote a song for me and for you.
It went: 'Tra la la
La la la la la tra.'
And sounded like that through and through.

Andrea Ward, Age 15, Park Dean School

There once was a young girl called Jill,
Whose good-looking boyfriend named Phil,
When he bought her a vase,
Plus a couple of cars,
Had the nerve then to send her the bill!

Matthew Loader, Age 11, Moseley Junior School

There was a young man from Stranraer,
Who attacked a young girl in his car.
Said she: 'Here's a wag!
I'm a fellow in drag!
So you see you won't get very far.'

David Hatch

I once gave a thirsty giraffe
A coconut just for a laugh.
I knew that he'd lack
The considerable knack
Of breaking it clean into half.

Colin West

There was an MP, name of Shoddy
Not even as clever as Noddy!
They transplanted a brain
But entirely in vain –
His new brain rejected his body.

Bob Monkhouse

There was a young man from Portmadoc
Who kept a strange beast in his paddock.
Though he fed it each day
With a great bale of hay,
It seemed to prefer a fresh haddock.

David Hatch

There was a young man called Blighty
Who wore a transparent nightie.
The vicar said, 'Son,
It's really not done,
It's not wrong – but it's also not rightie.'

Spike Milligan

There was a young chap called Maroo
Who never knew quite what to do.
He walked on his hands
And ate rubber bands,
And went to school in Peru.

Michael Palin

A fastidious chap, Cyril Pugh,
When visiting darkest Peru,
Took his bath and his toothbrush,
His sponge, and a blue-flush
Transistorized, pocket-sized loo.

Mick Gowar

There was a young lad named McCawl
Who went to a fancy dress ball.
He decided to risk it
And go as a biscuit,
But a dog ate him up in the hall.

Traditional

There was an old Member of Parliament for
North-East Cambridgeshire
Who was asked to write a limerick for a charity
which would aid blind children.
He said 'I don't understand
Why people should think I can write limericks
Simply because I received the votes of 26,936
people on June 9th 1983.

Clement Freud MP

There was a young man from New Delhi
Who kept all his cash in a welly.
But whoever he paid
Always said: 'I'm afraid
I can't take it. Your money's too smelly.'

Miles Kington

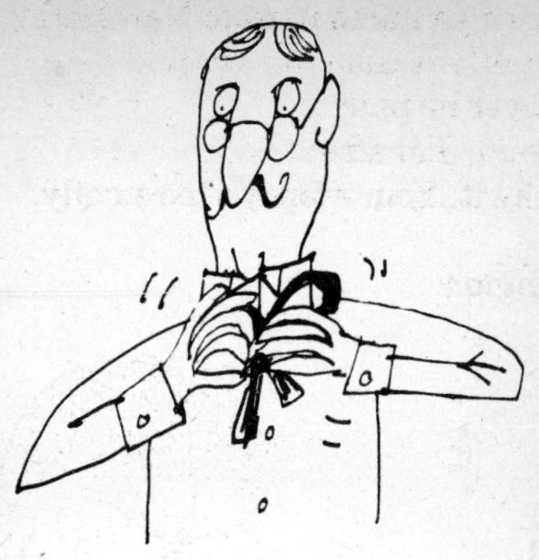

An elegant young Paraguayan
Was unable to keep his bow-tie on:
He tried lots and lots
Of remarkable knots,
But never found one to rely on.

Richard Heller

There was a young man from Bolivia
Who thought he was Laurence Olivier.
He acted Macbeth,
But his part died the death,
And the fans threw him into the rivier.

Richard Heller

There was a young lady called Freda
Who asked Schubert if ever he'd need her
To play or to dance:
'Not really,' said Franz.
'I'd rather you'd follow my Lieder. . . .'

Sir Michael Tippett

There was a young fellow called Tate,
Took his girl friend to dine at 8.08.
But I'd hate to relate
What that fellow called Tate,
And his tête-à-tête ate at eight eight.

Johnny Ball

A sharkling blin on the Glid
Went fracketing by in the nid
But the wiggles took fright
Nor a brolikill bite
And the tater was grunney well rid.

Spike Milligan

A wizard who lived at St Mary's
Had a castle haunted by fairies.
But one night with a wand,
Beside a small pond,
He changed them all to canaries.

George MacBeth

We are very depressed with our Yak,
Which has now become terribly slak.
It cleaned kitchens and stairs
Better than many au pairs,
So we're going to send our Yak bak.

Cyril Fletcher

An ostrich I met in Dundee,
Once ate a whole toolbox for tea,
Plus a radiogram,
A second-hand pram,
And a gumboot belonging to me.

Frank Muir

There was a young pilot from Bangor,
Who took a small plane from its hangar.
He flew it quite well
Till he hit the church bell,
When he dropped what you might call a clanger.

David Hatch

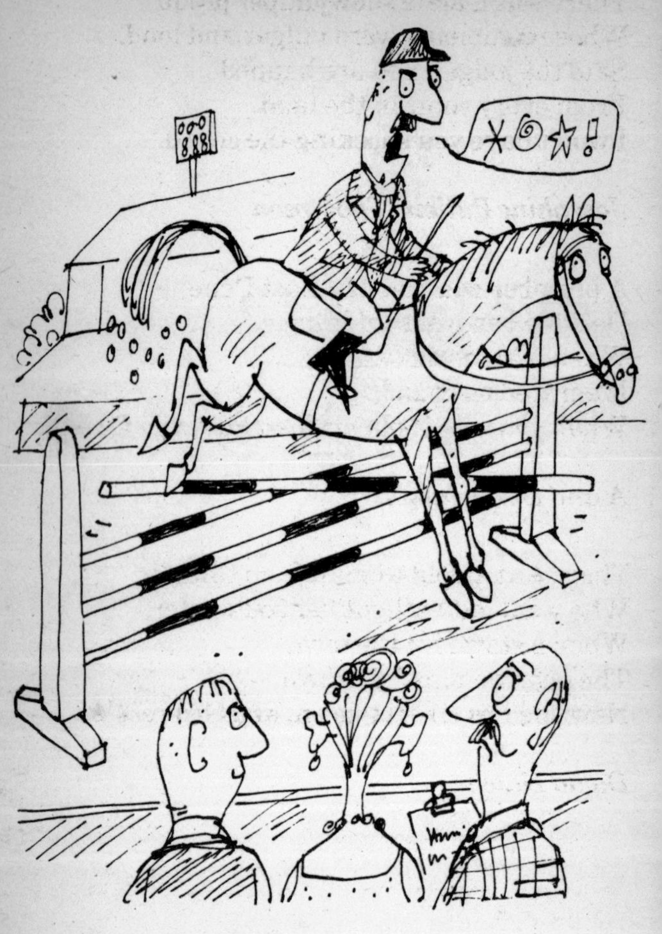

There was a male showjumper proud
Whose comments were vulgar and loud.
Said the judge: 'You are banned
From every show in the land.
I won't have you shocking the crowd.'

Josephine Pullein-Thompson

A plumber who lived in East Dene,
Designed an unusual latrine.
When seated you found
It emitted no sound;
When you rose it played 'God Save the Queen'.

A and D Newlands

There was an old woman from Chester
Who went out without her sou'wester;
When a storm hit the town,
The poor woman did drown,
Now she lies six feet down, and God rest 'er.

David Hatch

There was a young lady of Brom-i-ley
Who very soon mastered the homily:
'It is better by far
To rejoice at the barre
Than to be a dejected Sib-i-ley.'

Antoinette Sibley

A dancer arrived here from Spain –
Proud, dignified, lovely but vain.
When she came to appear,
Her dress showed a tear,
So she danced with but half of her train.

Beryl Grey

There was an old hag from Chicago,
Whose name was Amelia Virago.
Stowed away on a boat,
To the captain she wrote:
'The crew think I'm part of the cargo.'

Tony Whittome

An asthmatic old octogenarian
Went to Blackpool for the oxygen-in-the-air
  again.
On his first day in town
A green tram knocked him down.
Now he says he won't dare-to-go-there-again.

Traditional

There was a young lady named Riga
Who went for a ride on a tiger.
They came back from the ride
With the lady inside
And the smile on the face of the tiger.

Traditional

But what of her cousin named Ryon,
Who went for a ride on a lion,
Which ate all her clothes
From her head to her toes,
But left her her hankie to cry on?

Langford Reed

There once was a tartan balloon
Who blew all the way to the Moon.
Was he not a flier?
'I canna gang higher,
So I'll just turn roond and come D
O
O
N!'

Lavinia Derwent

Her husband once said to her: 'Florrie,
Your mouth is as big as a quarry!'
Then she opened it wide,
And there, right inside,
Was a man backing out in a lorry.

Bob Monkhouse

A balloonist competing from Cheshire
Had problems controlling the pressure.
As he sailed into space,
He lost touch with his race
And landed in South Eastern Asia.

David Frost

We quite liked the castle at Skipton,
Though the place was so wet we got dripped on.
There's a quaint old latrine
That was used by a queen –
Though they don't have the bed that she kipped on.

David Hatch

Mr Pudding from Yorkshire's West Riding
Bought a smart fallout shelter to hide in,
With a split-level hob
And posh seats on the bog –
But the day the Bomb dropped it just fried him.

Linda Hoy

(The moral is that Yorkshire puddings are best baked at a temperature of less than 5000°C.)

There was an old Bishop of Gloucester
Whose wife thought he chivvied and bossed her,
So she made him agree
To polyandry
And take the last place on her roster.

The Bishop of Gloucester

(Polyandry means to have many husbands.)

There once was an actor called Spam
Whose mouth buttoned up like a clam.
Said a man from his stall:
'I can't hear you at all –
You're not really a *Spam* but a *Ham*.'

Dame Peggy Ashcroft

There once was a writer from Stratford –
Thank God!

Ian McKellen

There was a young girl from Dorset
Whose mother wore a corset.
One day it did break
As she walked through the gate
So the young girl from Dorset enforced it.

Paula White, Age 16, Blatchington Court School

There was a young lady from Blaenau,
Who went for a ride on a rhino.
But when it dropped dead,
She ungraciously said:
'We could use this poor rhino for lino.'

David Hatch

When I was asked to write this poem
I went mad and thought I would show 'em
Now it's twenty past four:
I started five hours before
And still can't get the last line to rhyme!

Patrick W V White, Age 15,
Blatchington Court School

A man (of whose name I'm not sure)
Wrote rhymes every day by the score.
And though we would chorus:
'Your limericks bore us,'
He carried on writing still more. . . .

Colin West

ACKNOWLEDGEMENTS

Tom Baker and the publisher would like to thank Ms Joan Langford Reed for permission to use the limericks of Langford Reed in this anthology; Spike Milligan for limericks from *The 101 Best and Only Limericks of Spike Milligan* (Michael Joseph 1982); all the children from the Schools for the Blind who sent us in limericks; and everyone else who contributed to this anthology.

HELP A CHILD TO SEE

It is hard to understand fully what it is like to be blind for a child. It is difficult for anyone to cope with blindness, but perhaps the problems for children are even greater; and four out of ten blind children have another handicap as well.

The royalties from THE BOY WHO FORGOT TO GROW DOWN are being donated to the 'Help A Child To See' fund, which has been set up to raise £1,000,000 for a centre which not only cares for blind children, but also provides the opportunity for doctors to do more research into the disorders and illnesses which cause blindness in children, and to teach others about them.

The centre will be based at the Hospital for Sick Children, Great Ormond Street in London, but it will be open to children from all over the country. It will provide the care and treatment much needed by blind children, and will help doctors to find out more about the causes of their blindness and how to cure it.

You can help us raise the money we need for this centre. Only *one per cent* of the appeal target goes on administration costs, and the rest goes directly into the fund. If you would like to give anything, or find out more about the charity and how you can help, please write to us at this address:

'Help A Child To See'
Child Health Research Appeal Trust
Institute of Child Health
30 Guildford Street
LONDON
WC1N 1EH

David Taylor
'Help A Child To See'

NEVER WEAR YOUR WELLIES IN THE HOUSE

and other poems to make you laugh

Collected by Tom Baker

Here are some of the funniest poems you will ever read, written by some of the world's most popular poets and authors – including Spike Milligan, Jeremy Lloyd, Pam Ayres and Roald Dahl. All of the poems in this collection have been chosen by Tom Baker for one special reason: to make you laugh.

A royalty from every copy sold goes to the National Society for the Mentally Handicapped Child.

THE BROWNIE JOKE BOOK

Collected by Brownies

Why can't two elephants go for a swim together?
Because they've only got one pair of trunks between them.

Why are Brownies dizzy?
Because they're always doing good turns.

What is the cure for water on the knee?
Drainpipe trousers.

Brownies from all over the country have sent in their funniest jokes to make a book that will have you in fits. Elephant jokes, doctor jokes, food jokes, knock-knock jokes — every kind of joke that can possibly make you laugh is included in this hilarious collection.

THE FUNNIEST JOKE BOOK

Jim Eldridge

Just try to keep a straight face when you hear why the tonsils got dressed, what happens when you dial 666 and the fastest way to catch a squirrel. Here are hundreds of side-splitting jokes voted by children as the funniest they have ever heard.

NOT TO BE TAKEN SERIOUSLY

Colin West

Meet fat Wilhelmina, the ballerina, and obnoxious brother Bobby with his most revolting hobby, not to mention Kate who fell into a vat of dripping and Barbara who was gobbled up by a greedy bear at Scarborough.

The more than one-hundred verses in this riotous collection contain some of the most outrageous nonsense and hilarious advice you are ever likely to encounter.

THERESE BIRCH'S JELLYBONE GRAFFITI BOOK

For the first time – a collection of the best in graffiti, compiled by children for children.

Preserve wildlife – pickle a duck

Work fascinates me – I can sit and look at it for hours

Humpty Dumpty was pushed

Take an astronaut to launch

Sparrow has a whole nestful of exciting books that are available in bookshops or that you can order by post through the Sparrow Bookshop. Just complete the form below and enclose the money due and the books will be sent to you at home.

THE SECRET OF LOST LAKE	Carolyn Keene	95p	☐
THE WINKING RUBY MYSTERY	Carolyn Keene	£1.00	☐
THE GHOST IN THE GALLERY	Carolyn Keene	£1.00	☐
STAR TREK SHORT STORIES	William Rotsler	£1.25	☐
A PONY FOUND	D. Pullein-Thompson	95p	☐
SAVE THE PONIES	J. Pullein-Thompson	£1.25	☐
A NIGHT ON THUNDER ROCK	Enid Blyton	95p	☐
DRACULA	Bram Stoker	95p	☐

Humour

FUNNIEST JOKE BOOK	Jim Eldridge	£1.00	☐
BROWNIE JOKE BOOK	Compiled by Brownies	95p	☐
SCHOOL FOR LAUGHS	Peter Eldin	95p	☐
THE LAND OF UTTER NONSENSE	Colin West	£1.25	☐

And if you would like to hear more about our forthcoming books, write to the address below for the Beaver and Sparrow Bulletin.

SPARROW BOOKS, BOOKSERVICE BY POST, PO BOX 29, DOUGLAS, ISLE OF MAN, BRITISH ISLES.

Please enclose a cheque or postal order made out to Arrow Books Limited for the amount due including 15p per book for postage and packing for orders both within the UK and overseas orders.

Please print clearly

NAME ....

ADDRESS ....

....

Whilst every effort is made to keep prices down and popular books in print, Arrow Books cannot guarantee that prices will be the same as those advertised here or that the books will be available.

DEATH AND

Azul sighted ca[illegible] woman's dress was being ripped from her body.

The rifle bullet hit the man in the side as he got a grip on the cleavage of the blue dress. It went in through his ribs directly above the heart, tearing through that organ to glance off the right-side ribs and deflect upwards to produce a massive exit wound beneath the right arm. The man screamed once, torn sideways by the force of the close-range shot so that he pitched away, ultimately succeeding in ripping the dress clear of the woman's body. Beneath it, she was naked; the blood that fountained from the dead man's body splashed over her nubile breasts to induce a shriller scream that was followed by a shocked silence . . .

Other BREED novels by James A. Muir in Sphere Books:

THE LONELY HUNT
THE SILENT KILL
CRY FOR VENGEANCE
DEATH STAGE
THE GALLOWS TREE
THE JUDAS GOAT
TIME OF THE WOLF
BLOOD DEBT
BLOOD-STOCK
OUTLAW ROAD

BREED:

The Dying and the Damned

JAMES A. MUIR

SPHERE BOOKS LIMITED
30/32 Gray's Inn Road, London WC1X 8JL

First published in Great Britain by Sphere Books Ltd. 1980

They do pretty good, but there are some things a man just can't write around. This one is for Mizz Sue Fletcher.

TRADE
MARK

Set in Monotype Garamond

Printed in Great Britain by
William Collins Sons & Co Ltd
Glasgow

Chapter One

Azul levered the action of the Winchester and sighted carefully along the barrel.

It was a difficult shot because the woman was struggling so that the two men wrestling with her were in constant movement. One was clutching her around the waist while the other sought to rip her gingham dress loose from her body. The woman was screaming and kicking out, her flailing legs exposing calf-length riding boots and wide expanses of black-stockinged thigh. Her raven-dark hair was tumbled loose from the confining pins, fluttering as she shook her head so that the man holding her was partially blinded by the flying locks. The other was alternately grinning and cursing: enjoying the anticipation of rape, but reluctant to allow the preliminaries to last overlong.

Azul ended his frustration by squeezing the trigger.

The rifle bullet hit the man in the side as he got a grip on the cleavage of the blue dress. It went through his ribs directly above the heart, tearing through that organ to glance off the right-side ribs and deflect upwards to produce a massive exit wound beneath the right arm. The man screamed once, torn sideways by the force of the close-range shot so that he pitched away, ultimately succeeding in ripping the dress clear of the woman's body. Beneath it, she was naked; the blood that fountained from the dead man's body splashed over her nubile breasts to induce a shriller scream that was followed by a shocked silence.

The second man let go her waist and reached for the Remington Army model holstered on his right hip. Azul shot him as the hand closed on the butt of the pistol, aiming for the head to avoid the falling woman. The ·44-40 slug entered the face as the man turned, ploughing into his right eye and coming out behind his left ear on a massive wash of bloodied bone and sticky grey brain matter. The man twisted and fell down with his mouth open and his hand clenched tight on the pistol.

Azul levered a fresh shell into the breech and waited, ingrained Apache caution dictating that he be sure of his prey before exposing himself.

Neither man moved. Nor was there sign of any others: only the corpses and the two women.

The dark-haired woman lifted up on her knees, simultaneously scrubbing at her blood-drenched breasts and trying to hide them. The older woman turned her face towards the trees, straining against the ropes that bound her to the wagon's wheel. She was a good twenty years senior, her hair mostly grey, dragged back in a tight bun that emphasised the firm set of her features. Once, she had been beautiful, and the memory lingered on despite the wrinkles and the bruises that decorated her mouth and eyes. She was dressed in black – widow's weeds – but cut to accentuate the fullness of her figure, the still-young slenderness of her waist. It looked – as best the halfbreed could tell – to be an expensive dress.

Her voice was hoarse, as though scoured by shouting, but her blue eyes were clear as she scanned the trees.

'Thanks! You gonna show yourself?' Then: 'Grace! For decency's sake get yourself covered up!'

The younger woman – Grace – went on sobbing and scrubbing at her body.

Azul came out from the trees, moving warily, his eyes scanning the surrounding hills like a cautious mountain lion moving in on a wounded animal.

The two women saw a tall man, a mane of tangled blond hair falling to his shoulders from beneath a flat-crowned, black stetson. A shirt that had once been white and was now the colour of curdled cream from sweat and wear and washing opened halfway down a muscular chest. A leather vest covered the shirt, a gunbelt that held a Colt's Frontier model on the right hip and a Bowie knife sheathed on the left. The shirt was tucked into buckskin pants, aged by wear, themselves tucked inside knee-high Chiricahua moccasins, the right moccasin showing the wooden handle of a throwing knife that was sheathed against his leg. His eyes were blue, as much Anglo-Saxon as his hair; but his face was Indian: Apache, or a mixture of the two races. Wide cheekbones matched a slightly flattened nose, the square jaw sporting a wide, full-lipped mouth that was now drawn out thin as he waited for danger, easing into a smile only when he was confident of his own safety.

He lowered the hammer of the Winchester and paced across the clearing. The woman called Grace stilled her sobbing, tugging up the remnants of her dress to cover her naked body.

Azul drew the Bowie knife and hacked through the cords binding the older woman to the wheel. She staggered as she came free, then forced herself upright, rubbing at the welts on her wrists.

'Thanks, mister.' When she smiled a whole lot of her youth came back to her face. 'You saved my daughter from a fate worse'n death.'

Azul shrugged. 'Is there one? What were they doing?'

'My God!' The younger woman spoke for the first time. 'I'd have thought that was obvious even to a halfbreed.'

'Grace! You still that tongue!' The older woman's voice cut like a whip's lash through the sudden silence. 'This gentleman saved us both. You acknowledge that fact and thank him. Now!'

Suddenly, the girl turned to face Azul, and he saw that she was even better looking at close range, her black hair framing an oval of sun-tanned face in which were set large green eyes and a generous, sensual mouth that, even devoid of lipstick, was red; enticing.

'Sorry, momma.' She stood up, holding the dress tight

against her full body. 'Sorry, mister. And thanks.'

'Pleasure,' grunted Azul. 'At least for some.'

He ducked his head at the two bodies and the older woman moved fast to answer his unspoken question.

'They jumped us and killed our driver.' She pointed past the restive six-mule team to where a crumbled body stretched on the winter grass . The grass was bright red all around the corpse. 'They was fixing to rape my daughter, then kill us both. It was real lucky you came along.'

Azul nodded without speaking.

'Fact is,' the woman continued, 'we're headed for Wyoming. My brother's got some land on the Montana side and we was going to join him. My name's Hope Walls, by the way. That's my daughter, Grace.'

'Ladies.' Azul touched his hat. 'What you aim to do now?'

'Carry on.' Hope Walls's face set in determined lines. 'My husband got killed a few months back and since then we've been planning this trip.'

Azul's knowledge of geography was sketchy, limited to what his white father had been able to teach him, but he felt sure that Wyoming was a long way northwards. He knew that they were now in Apacheria – a part designated the New Mexico Territory by the white men – and that Wyoming was many miles distant. Beyond that, his knowledge was vague.

'How will you get there?' he asked. 'Now your driver's dead?'

'We got a map,' said Hope Walls. 'And I've handled a team before.'

'Handling a team's not the same as handling men,' murmured the halfbreed. 'You just saw that.'

'We've got guns.' Grace Walls moved past him, both arms wrapped across her bosom. 'We can look after ourselves.'

'Yeah,' Azul grunted. 'Sure you can.'

Grace blushed, trying to climb over the tailboard of the wagon and hold her dress in place at the same time. It was a hopeless task, and as she finally managed to clamber across the upright board, her dress fell away, revealing the firm mounds of her bosom.

'He's got a point,' said her mother. 'We need a man along to handle things like this.'

She turned to stare at Azul.

'I'll pay you five hundred dollars if you're the man. Two hundred right now and the rest when we reach where we're headed.'

Azul cradled the Winchester, thinking about it. He had money in his saddlebags from the killing of the Nillson gang*, but he was still posted around the Border so a sojourn in the north wouldn't hurt overmuch. Might even allow old memories to die down. He nodded.

'All right.'

'Good.' Hope Walls stuck her hand out. 'You got a deal. Wait until Grace gets herself dressed again and I'll fetch the money out.'

'Sure.' Azul turned away, going back amongst the trees to bring his horse out from where he had left the animal when he first heard the screaming.

He led the big grey stallion into the clearing and tethered the part-Arab to the wagon. Then he walked over to the driver's body and turned the corpse on its back. The man had been shot three times, twice in the chest and once in the face. Whatever he had looked like before, he was now unrecognisable: just a pot-bellied hunk of meat for the coyotes and the buzzards. Azul went to check the other bodies. The man who had been holding Grace wore a gunbelt with cartridges slotted along its length. They were of a calibre that fitted the halfbreed's rifle, so he emptied them into his hat and stowed them in his saddlebags. The other man wore a ·36 calibre Colt, a conversion of the old Navy model, the shells useless to Azul. Their pockets revealed little more than a few dollars – which he folded and tucked inside his vest – and the kind of personal momentoes men carry with them:

* *See: BREED 10 – OUTLAW ROAD*

a faded picture of a half-naked woman; a tag from a San Antonio brothel; a letter from someone called Agatha, exhorting her son to lead a good life. The letter was old, faded by sun and much reading, the folds fraying into holes at the corners.

The men had left their horses to the side of the clearing. Both carried sheathed Winchesters on the saddles and boxes of cartridges in the bags. Azul transferred the carbines to the wagon along with the shells, then went back to rummage through the saddlebags. He found an array of dirty underwear, a pair of clean shirts, some dried food and a letter.

The letter carried no date or name, only the message: *They will head for Bandera. If you can halt their journey I would pay you the agreed sum on delivery.*

It was unsigned.

Azul crumpled it and thrust it back inside the saddlebag.

Grace Walls emerged from the wagon clad in a pink dress. She shrieked. 'My God! Momma! He's looting them! He's robbing the bodies!'

The halfbreed unhitched the two horses and walked them over to tether them behind the wagon. One was a handsome roan stallion, the other a piebald gelding. He smiled at Grace.

'Should I leave them there? Let the coyotes take them? Or let them starve to death?'

'God!' Grace shuddered. 'That's like robbing a grave.'

'I never done that,' murmured Azul, 'but I never seen the point of leaving dead men stuff living folks might use.'

'But you're stealing from the dead.'

'Beats stealing from the living.'

'He's right.' Hope Walls pushed her daughter aside and climbed down from the tailgate. 'Those guns might be useful to us. And don't forget what those men tried to do to you. Taking their horses is just a fair exchange.'

Grace shuddered some more, but held her mouth tight shut. Azul grinned and said, 'The horses should fetch about twenty-five dollars each. Reckon the saddles are worth twice that. We'll split the difference when we reach Bandera.'

Abruptly, he realised that was the town named in the letter. He tugged it out and passed it to Hope.

'That mean anything to you, ma'am?'

Hope Walls shook her head. 'No. Nothing at all. I can't imagine what it means.'

Azul shrugged and hitched his own horse alongside the others. Then he climbed into the seat of the wagon and whooped the mules up from their grazing, heading towards Bandera.

They reached Bandera in the late afternoon, just as the sun began to hide itself behind the distant bulk of the Mogallons. Grace stayed silent throughout the ride, though her mother explained the purpose of their journey.

She had been married to a man called Jeremiah Walls who ran a small silver mine just south of the Border. When her husband got killed in a fight over a hand of poker, she had sold up her interest in the mine and sent word to her brother, Joshua, in Wyoming. Joshua had apparently begun business as a trader and then built a whole town around his post. The town was called – aptly – Jericho, and Joshua owned most of it. He had promised Hope and her daughter a home there, so they had stacked whatever they felt worth keeping on to the wagon and headed north.

Azul accepted the story for want of reasons to question it, though something about it sounded wrong.

He forgot his doubts as they entered Bandera.

The town was little more than a straggle of adobe shacks and wooden houses spread along a dusty trail. A windmill swung lazily at one end of the street, pumping a trickle of oily water into a catch tank; a church stood at the other end. In between there was a saloon, a livery stable, a dry goods store, a hardware store, and a stage office. That was all.

Azul pointed at the stage office and said, 'Might be easier if you went north with Wells Fargo.'

Hope Walls looked at her daughter and then shook her head. 'No. All we own is in this wagon. We're not leaving it.'

'Your decision, ma'am.' Azul eased the mules to a halt outside the saloon. 'I'll go check if they got rooms for you.'

He climbed down and walked into the saloon. It was small and dark and dirty, the light dim even though the setting sun was shining full on the windows. Apart from the barkeep, only three men were inside. Two looked like cowhands eking out their last few dollars over a bottle of whisky; the other was a gambler, idly shuffling cards across a baize-topped table.

Azul went up to the bar and asked for beer. It came in a glass mug, tepid and half froth. The halfbreed looked at the bartender. The bartender looked back. Azul asked for a spoon, and then scooped the foam clear of the liquid, shoving the mug back across the counter.

'Now give me a beer I can drink.'

'We don't generally serve 'breeds.' The barkeep ignored the glass. 'You're lucky to get anythin' at all.'

Azul nodded. 'I didn't know that. I guess there's an apology due.'

'Yeah.' The barkeep grinned, sucking in his gut and trying hard to transfer the weight to his chest. 'I guess there is.'

'From you,' said Azul. Quietly.

'What the hell you talkin' about?' The barkeep was around fifty, his hair thin under its layer of pomade, his face pale around watery brown eyes. 'If business were better you wouldn't even get in here.'

'Trouble is,' said Azul, 'that I'm in.'

He lifted the mug and flung the contents in the man's face. The beer splashed into the barkeep's eyes. Ran down his flabby cheeks to mingle with the wax holding his moustache in place. It was a very fine moustache: a compensation for the lack of hair on his head. It was grown long and waxed into curls on either side of his mouth, the twisted points curving back almost to his nostrils. The beer washed the wax out so that the curls flattened, turning the moustache downwards.

The bartender gasped and dropped his hands under the counter.

Azul reached forwards with his left hand, grabbing a fistful of shirtfront to drag the man forwards across the bar. At the same time he brought his right hand forwards. It was still holding the empty mug.

The glass shattered against the barkeep's face, shards of glass mashing into his cheeks and lips. His sallow face was suddenly dark with spilling blood, and his shout became a high-pitched scream of pain. Azul twisted the mug, grinding the shattered fragments of glass deep into the pain-racked face. He let go of the man's shirt as the bloody mouth opened to spill a column of vomit over the bar. The bartender fell back, both hands pressed tight against his face. Then screamed again as his probing fingers drove the pieces of the broken mug deeper into his flesh.

Azul dropped the mug and turned to face the other drinkers. Instinctively, his right hand moved towards the Colt on his hip. No one moved. The gambler just went on shuffling his deck and the two cowboys went back to their drinking. Azul reached over the bar, fumbling round until he located the familiar contours of a shotgun. He lifted the weapon clear: it was a Meteor twin-barrel, cut down to around nine inches. He broke the ugly weapon open and thumbed the shells clear. Then tossed it over to the far wall. He threw the shells in the opposite direction. Then spun round, drawing his Colt as the bat-wing doors opened.

'Use that and you'll never get the final payment.'

Hope Walls stood just inside the doors with a Remington scattergun cocked on both hammers in her hands.

Azul nodded, holstering the Colt.

'What's going on?' demanded the woman. 'We heard a lot of shouting. Sounded like a fight was started.'

'No contest,' murmured Azul. 'I just got served some

rotten beer, but the barkeep didn't agree. I made him eat his words.'

The barkeep chose that moment to drag himself up from the floor. The entire lower half of his face was a mash of red, from just under his eyes to the point of his dimpled chin. He was still plucking pieces of glass from his face.

'I think,' announced Hope Walls, 'that we should seek accommodation elsewhere. Perhaps the stage depot can offer us rooms.'

'If you're with him you goddam better look someplace else,' mumbled the barkeep. 'You ain't stayin' here.'

The grey-haired woman glanced around the saloon, then nodded. 'Don't believe I'd want to if you serve beer that bad.'

Azul grinned and followed Hope out of the saloon.

'He might stir up some trouble, ma'am. But thanks for backing me.'

'You're an investment,' said the old lady. 'You already invested two men, so I want you around. Call it an insurance.'

Azul laughed and stepped off the sidewalk into the dust that filled the street. He grabbed the harness of the lead mule and turned the team around, back in the direction of the stage office.

There were no rooms available at the depot, so they slept in the stable. That, at least, was warm and quiet, the silence disturbed only by the shuffling of the mules as they moved about their stalls and dragged mouthfuls of fodder from the mangers. Azul slept easily, enjoying the luxury of a straw bed after long weeks on the trail. The two women elected to sleep inside the wagon, even though the owner of the stable insisted on charging them an extra dollar for bringing the big conestoga inside.

In the morning they moved the wagon out and cooked their own breakfast. The two Walls were equipped with money if nothing else, so Grace went off to buy eggs and dry provisions while her mother, with Azul's help, got a fire started. They ate bacon and fried eggs, along with corn-bread and canned beans. The ostler bought the roan stallion and the piebald gelding for thirty dollars apiece after a degree of haggling; and the two saddles were sold for a total amount of seventy-five dollars.

Azul took half and they moved out at noon.

The last thing they saw of Bandera was the barkeep, his face swathed in bandages and his fist shaking. Only Azul caught the words from under the cloth.

'They'll find you. I swear they'll find you. I'll tell them where you're headed.'

'What's he mean?' Azul asked Hope. 'What's he talking about?'

'I don't know.' The grey-haired woman shrugged and turned away. 'Just upset, I guess.'

'Yeah.' Azul was doubtful. 'He's got reason to feel cut up.'

Chapter Two

Out from Bandera the land lifted again into a series of sway-back ridges that were thick with pine and aspen. The air was chill, though a moist breeze carried a hint of the approaching spring, and the first inkling of fresh growth was beginning to show on the bare trees. The map Hope Walls showed the halfbreed indicated a trail that led more or less due north, skirting around Albuquerque to touch Santa Fe before moving on along the eastern edge of the hills into Colorado. Grace stayed mostly inside the wagon, trying to read a book as the conestoga shuddered and slid over the winter-damp ground. Hope remained beside Azul on the seat, one of the Winchesters canted across her knees.

'I forgot to ask your name,' she said. 'Guess it must have been the excitement.'

'Matthew Gunn.' He kept his eyes on the trail ahead. 'Or Azul.'

'That's Spanish for blue, ain't it?' Hope queried. 'How come you got two names?'

Azul grinned, omitting to mention that he was – perhaps – best known by the nickname he had picked up around the Border: Breed.

'My pa was white. Man called Kieron Gunn. He married an Apache woman, so I got a name from both sides. My pa got me christened in Santa Fe, but the Chiricahua named me Azul. On account of my eyes.'

'A halfbreed.' Grace had given up her attempt at reading and was listening to their conversation. 'I told you, momma. He's probably going to trade us off to his Apache friends.'

'Headed the wrong way for that,' grunted Azul. 'There's

slaves sold down around the Border, but mostly by Comancheros. To Mexicans. Most of the slaves are Apache. The Mexicans use the women and the children in the cotton fields, or as servants. Offer a bounty on the men's scalps.'

The coldness in his voice hushed Grace, warning her that she was touching on a painful – and potentially dangerous – subject. In turn, Azul felt a shadow creep over his mind. His parents, along with the whole of his *rancheria* had been killed by scalphunters, and since finding the mutilated bodies he had spent some years tracking down and killing the murderers. It was that lonely hunt that had given him the reputation of a cold-bloodied killer, and the name of Breed*.

'I trust him.' Hope Walls made the statement very final, her tone cutting off the protests of her daughter. She turned to Azul: 'What should we call you?'

He shrugged. 'Don't make much difference, ma'am. You choose it.'

'We shall call you Azul. That has a nice ring to it. You may call me Hope, and my daughter, Grace. After all we shall be riding together for a long time.'

'Yeah,' said Azul, concentrating on the trail.

Several things worried him about the journey, but as yet he could not fit them together into a coherent pattern.

The enormous distance the two women had elected to travel was the first oddity. They could have reached the Wyoming border by stage coach, along with a few wagon-borne journeys, far safer – and far quicker – than by this overland route. Their insistence on using the wagon was odd. It was uncomfortable and dangerous, yet they had already expressed a firm resolve to travel by conestoga.

At the same time, the wagon was unusually heavy. Azul was not accustomed to handling a mule team, but he knew – from his father – that mules were exceptionally powerful animals. Slow, maybe, but very strong. This team was labouring on the up-grades. The interior of the wagon was

* *See BREED nos. 1–10*

loaded up with a mass of furniture, ranging from stacked chairs to a spinola, and consequently very heavy. But even so, the team was making heavy going.

Then there was the letter he had found in the rapists' saddlebags. On its own, it might not mean anything, but it had mentioned Bandera. And in the town, the cut-up barkeep had shouted something about *telling them where you're headed.*

None of it added up. At least not into an identifiable pattern, so he decided to wait and watch and listen.

They halted at noon to rest the team and prepare food. Azul scouted the terrain ahead and around their position, finding it empty of threat, so that he squatted down to eat the beans and beef the women had cooked with a clear conscience.

Grace remained distant, though her mother talked freely of her dead husband's mine and the problems of living in Mexico. Azul listened with half his attention, wondering why a woman as attractive as Grace Walls remained unwed. The question stayed unanswered in his mind as they kicked dirt over the fire and stowed the plates back inside the wagon.

They moved on, following the course of the Rio Grande as the big river cut its way through the hills, providing a trail that was relatively easy to follow.

They hit a length of ground that was mostly flat: a long ridge running beside the mountains for several miles, some primeval upsurge of the soil allowing a natural terrace to flank the river. Azul passed the guidelines of the mule team to Hope and unhitched the grey stallion from the rear of the wagon. Then he mounted and rode on ahead.

As he turned a bend the wind changed, bringing to his attuned ears the remnants of a conversation.

'He's going . . .' It was Grace's voice. 'You know that . . . Got his two hundred . . . Won't see him again . . . Can't trust a man . . .'

'Wait . . .' Now Hope spoke. 'He saved us . . . Seems decent . . . What else?'

Azul lost the threads as he turned the corner and urged the big grey up a fall of rock that gave access to the upper levels of the ridge. He rode the stallion up to the starting point of the slide and then turned the animal southwards. The same kind of doubts that clouded his thinking about the Walls women's journey north prompted him to check their back trail. But after one hour's ride through the trees he had still not picked up any sign of pursuit, so he turned the horse around and hurried to check the forward trail. There was no sign of ambush ahead, and he began to wonder if he was being overly cautious.

It was early evening before he rejoined the wagon, having found a suitable camping place a mile or so ahead.

'Well?' Hope Walls was handling the team while her daughter sat beside her, a Winchester clutched nervously in her hands. 'Find anything?'

'Place to stop the night was all.' Azul reined in the grey and turned the stallion to match the direction of the mules. 'Best I can tell, there's nobody following us, nor nobody in front.'

'Well.' Grace sniffed and lowered the carbine. 'If a half-breed can't find tracks, who can?'

'Grace!' Her mother turned. 'I'll not tell you again! Just watch your tongue.' She turned to Azul: 'I'm sorry. My daughter is a little overwrought.'

Azul nodded, muttering, 'Maybe that's why she's not married.'

Which was another part of the unanswerable puzzle: Grace was an attractive woman. And *woman*, rather than *girl*. She was close on thirty, if not already there, but still single. In a country where girls married young, their chances enhanced by beauty and family money, Grace was a curiosity. She should have been wed, even had a child or two. Instead, she was obviously single, her fingers devoid of rings; nor was there hint of a ring having ever encircled her finger.

The halfbreed pushed the thoughts from his mind, concentrating on the trail. He rode out in front, leading the wagon down towards the spot he had picked out.

It was a spur of land that stuck out into the river where a landslide had dumped stone into the water, forcing the Rio Grande to divert its course and flow around the base of hard rock. Earth had fallen alongside the stone, and grass had grown there, followed later by trees. The overall result was that a kind of island jutted out into the river with a thick covering of grass and aspens providing a screen from the wind. It was as sweet a camping spot as any Azul had seen.

They took the wagon down on to the spur and turned the mules loose, hobbling each animal before allowing it to crop at the still-verdant grass. Azul unsaddled the grey stallion and looped a rawhide cord about the forelimbs. As an extra precaution he swung a rope across the narrow entrance to the spur, fastening the ends to the willows that grew either side, their drooping limbs reaching down into the water. The trees made an effective screen for the fire the two women built, and as the sun disappeared behind the rimrock they settled down to a meal.

As had become usual, Hope made the conversation, Grace remaining silent. Azul contributed no more than was the bare necessity that kept the talk going.

'What do you believe is our best route, Azul?' Hope stared at the map. 'You know this area, don't you?'

The halfbreed shrugged. 'As far as Trinidad. That's all. Beyond there is anyone's guess.'

Grace snorted and Hope studied the map. 'Trinidad. Ah, yes. That's just over the New Mexico line, in Colorado.'

'It's on the old Santa Fe route,' said Azul. 'My pa took me up that way once. Beyond there I don't know the country.'

'Perhaps we should discharge Mr Gunn there,' suggested Grace, acidly. 'A driver who doesn't know the country can't be much use.'

'He was use enough when those two were fixing to spread your legs,' snapped Hope. 'I didn't hear no arguments from you then.'

'Men!' was all Grace answered.

Azul just grinned and emptied his coffee. 'Best bed down now. I'll sleep by the neck.'

He picked up his bedroll and saddle, and strolled over to where the rope was stretched across the narrow causeway leading to the 'island'. He checked the animals and then spread his blanket on the ground under a thick stand of aspens. He stretched out, fully clothed, with the Winchester cradled in his arms. Sleep came fast, but not before he caught the sound of the two women arguing. He couldn't make out the exact words, but he thought it was all over him. He grinned, feeling vaguely amused, then allowed himself to drift into a shallow sleep.

He woke several times during the night. Once when a wolf howled, then again when a bluejay screamed, its own rest disturbed by some marauding predator; again when the mules snickered a warning at an approaching bobcat that spat and snarled before racing off through the trees flanking the upper levels of the river valley. Each time the sounds registered on his mind while he was still part-way unconscious and he returned to sleep when his instinct told him there was no real danger. It was a habit he had learned as a child, living amongst the Chiricahua Apache, one that was honed finer by lessons learnt on the war trail, and finally tuned to its current level by the need to stay alive in the face of multiple threats.

Old Sees-The-Fox, the Chiricahua hunter, had told him one time that no warrior could afford to sleep like a white man.

Sleep with one eye open, he had told the young warrior, *and one ear listening. That way you stay alive longer. The only time a fighting man can afford to sleep like others is when he knows he is safe amongst friends, with a guard at his door.*

It was one of the reasons most Indians kept dogs and horses around their tepees, and why many of the Plains Indians would sleep with the bridle of their best pony lashed to their wrist or ankle.

The years of Apache training had taught Azul to sleep like

that, ready to wake at the slightest sound whilst still recouping the energy spent during the day. He was now accustomed to sleeping in the saddle, or to grabbing a cat-nap when the opportunity offered; at the same time remaining alert so that the difference between rest and full awakening was minimal.

He came fully awake at dawn, even though the sun was not yet shining into the wide bed of the river, its light confined to the upper reaches of the western hills. He rolled clear of his blanket and scanned the surrounding terrain, then checked the mules and his own horse, feeding them a small measure of oats before blowing the fire into fresh life. He set the coffee pot over the flames and then drifted through the trees on the south side of the 'island' to where a beach of shale flanked the spur of land.

He set his guns down on the gravel and stripped out of his clothes before plunging into the water. The river was icy cold and he stayed in the water only long enough to cleanse his body. Along with many of the other myths concocted by the white man was that which said Indians were dirty. It was a fallacy: most Indians washed as often as they could, often more frequently than their detractors. Dirt and sweat were things they could live with when the need arose, but things they preferred not to have when bathing facilities were available.

Azul scrubbed his body with sand that he lifted from the river bed and then dried himself on his blanket, spreading the square of cloth out where the early sun would dry it fast. Then he got dressed and poured a cup of coffee.

The smell woke the women, and for a while there was a scrabble of movement inside the conestoga. Then Hope emerged, fully dressed, followed by Grace.

The older woman saw Azul's wet hair and asked, 'Where'd you get washed up so clean?'

The halfbreed pointed at the river. 'It's cold, but the water's fresh.'

'I could use a bath.' She turned to her daughter. 'Where'd we stow those towels?'

'Momma!' Grace sounded outraged. 'You can't think of bathing here. What about him?'

She pointed at Azul.

'I think he might just be gentleman enough to turn his back,' said Hope. 'And I'm itching something awful from that stable. Go fetch the towels and we'll dip together.'

'Momma!'

Azul stood up. 'I'll scout ahead. Check the trail in front. Maybe you'll have breakfast ready when I get back.'

He saddled the big part-Arab and then loosened the rope closing off the neck of land. He coiled it and looped it back over his saddlehorn. Then mounted and turned to face the women.

'Stay quiet, but if anything happens – yell. I'll not be far away.'

As he crossed the causeway he caught the tail-end of Grace's comment: 'Means he'll be watching us. Up there. Waiting for us to take our clothes off.'

He was on the point of riding back when Hope's voice sounded through the trees. It might have been that she was genuinely ashamed of her daughter's suspicions, or simply that she was angry. To Azul it didn't really matter.

'Don't be so foolish, girl. He's proved himself a friend, and you owe him. If he wanted to watch you, he needn't have gone off like that. Now: you want to bathe, or not?'

Azul rode up to the trail and checked the land ahead, then circled round to check the back trail. The country was empty of anything but animals. He saw the tracks of the bobcat he had heard in the night and the deeper pad marks of a cougar; a bluejay screamed at him and a flight of ravens took off from a patch of wild corn as he approached; he saw a skunk go running through the trees, and watched a group of squirrels flow limber through the branches of the pines. Of men, white or red, there was no sign.

He turned back, listening to the squeals of the women as they splashed in the river. Deliberately, he reined in and waited until the squealing stopped, then he rode forwards, making a whole lot of unnecessary noise.

By the time he reached the finger of rock, Hope was busy over the fire and Grace was inside the wagon. Azul dismounted, his mouth watering at the smell of frying bacon and the sizzle of eggs.

'You were right about the river.' The grey-haired woman looked up smiling. 'And right about Grace. How come you're so tactful?'

'Natural charm.' Azul grinned, hitching the big grey to a tree. 'I reckoned you had some talking to do.'

'Don't pay overmuch attention to Grace.' Hope Walls looked up from the pan. 'She got badly let down once and that kind of soured her to men.'

'You talking about me, momma?'

Grace emerged from the wagon. Her hair was still slick from the water so that it shone like a raven's wing, tugged back from her face into a pony's tail that was gathered by a blue ribbon the same colour as her dress. Her face was flushed – whether from the cold dip or embarrassment, Azul could not tell – and her eyes sparkled. She clutched a shawl about her shoulders, trembling slightly in the early chill, the woollen material hiding the cleavage of the dress.

'Just saying you took a bath, honey.' Hope glanced at Azul in confirmation. 'And that you enjoyed it.'

'I like to keep clean.' Grace spoke to her mother, avoiding Azul's eyes. 'Same as other folks. But I'm more used to real bath-houses.'

'They don't build too many out here,' murmured the half-breed. 'You just take what you find.'

Hope quelled any further comment by the simple expedient of doling out the food.

They ate in silence, then Azul got the mules back in the traces while the two women cleaned the plates and stowed their gear inside the wagon. Hope volunteered to drive so as to leave Azul free to check the trail ahead, and Grace climbed up on the seat beside her mother. Azul paced the grey out a quarter mile ahead, halting every so often to check that the wagon was keeping pace. From where he sat, Hope looked like a skilled teamster, swinging the mules almost casually around the obstacles and curves of the winding trail.

The only discordant note was struck by Grace. Once the sun had climbed over the eastern edge of the river valley it struck warmth into the bottomlands and she let the shawl slide from her shoulders. Her dress was a dark blue, silky, with an iridescent sheen. The skirt was full, exposing a froth of petticoats; it was nipped in at the waist and above, whalebone angled the cleavage upwards so that Grace's breasts were lifted and firmed. The neckline was low, more suitable to a saloon or some fancy *salon* than to a wagon trip along the edge of the Sangre de Cristo range.

It was another piece in the puzzle of doubt building around the two women.

For the next seven days Hope Walls continued to wear the same black dress she had on when Azul first saw her tied to the wagon wheel. Grace produced a fresh garment each morning, some demure, but most looking more like ball gowns than travel clothes. Azul said nothing, though curiosity bit at his mind like rats nibbling on a sack of grain.

So far, it didn't matter much, because the land was empty and there was no one to see the exciting sight of the lovely woman. But soon they would reach Santa Fe, and there Grace's dresses might excite something more than casual interest.

The last night on the trail before reaching the city, Azul mentioned the dresses. To Hope.

'I know,' said the older woman. 'I'll talk to her.'

She turned away, setting a full stop on the conversation that Azul felt wary of breaking. In the morning Grace appeared in a demure blouse, buttoned high at the neck and topped with a tiny string tie. She wore a plain skirt of brown cloth, ankle length, with high-heeled boots on her feet. In an odd kind of way, the outfit was even more exciting than the sophisticated dresses she had worn previously.

Azul dismissed the thought, concentrating on leading the wagon in to the city. It had been a long time since he had visited Santa Fe, and the place had grown during that time. He reined in, waiting for the wagon to catch up, then pointed at the city.

'Santa Fe.' He remembered the doubts, adding, 'I hope there won't be anyone waiting for you there.'

A look of surprise crossed Hope Walls's face, quickly hidden behind a bright smile. 'Why should there be?'

Azul shrugged. 'I don't know. But if there could be, you might tell me now.'

'Evil is where you find it, Mister Gunn.' Grace smiled primly. 'What reason could there be for anyone to harm us?'

'Like the saying,' rasped Azul. 'See no evil, hear no evil. Then it hits you an' you got no choice but to feel it.'

'I am sure we shall not feel anything,' said Grace.

Azul looked at her and grinned. 'Up to you, ma'am.'

Chapter Three

Santa Fe spread before them, the southern perimeter of the city bounded by the tracks of the Atchison, Topeka and Santa Fe railroad. Stockyards and loading bays flanked the rails, and three massive locomotives stood like sullen animals in the sidings. Azul led the wagon past the rail tracks and the shanties surrounding the depot into the old town. Here there were wide avenues of houses that showed the mixed influences that had built the city. Whitewashed buildings with wrought-iron covering the windows and high surrounding walls indicated the Spanish influence, while alongside stood houses of brick and timber that marked the steady growth of the American presence in what had begun as a Mexican town.

It was around noon, and the streets were quiet, the odours of cooking permeating the air as they traversed the tree-lined avenues. The streets were neat, set out on a grid pattern that focused on the central plaza. This great square was bounded on one side by the cathedral where Kieron Gunn had brought his son to be christened, along the remaining three sides there were administrative buildings and saloons. The start of the Old Spanish Trail, to the west, was now a wide thoroughfare lined by stores, hotels, eating houses, and more saloons. The main street was extended off to the west, its businesses the same as the facing roadway.

Here, the buildings were two and three storeys high, some even going up to a fourth floor. Buckboards and wagons and more decorous carriages filled the streets, moving slower than the mounted men weaving their horses through the bustle of four- and two-wheeled vehicles. Hope Walls turned the wagon ponderously into the flow of traffic, circling the plaza as Azul pointed to the western edge. He spotted a livery stable flanking a street wide enough to take the wagon and shouted for the women to wait as he checked the rear. There was a corral in back of the main barn, so he waved the wagon into the street, dismounting to unlatch the gate. As he swung the heavy timbers inwards, a man with a limp emerged from the rear of the stable, his face frowning a question.

'Got a wagon,' Azul called. 'Want to put up for a night or two.'

The man limped closer, revealing himself as younger than his prematurely grey hair suggested. His face was thin, as though pinched in by pain, and the halfbreed noticed that he winced each time he set his damaged leg down.

'Shit! A conestoga.' The down-turned mouth lifted into a thin-lipped smile. 'I ain't seen a conestoga in years.'

He shuffled forwards to take the bridle of the left-side lead mule, turning the animal adroitly into the corral. Azul swung the gate closed on the wagon and slotted the latch back in place.

'Ma'am.' The stablehand made it a general greeting to both women. 'You come far?'

'Far enough,' replied Hope. 'Will the wagon be safe here?'

'Someone on duty all the time.' The man began to unharness the team. 'Where you headed?'

'North.' The grey-haired woman remained guarded. 'Up Wyoming way.'

'Long stretch.' The man offered his hand to Grace. 'Indian country up that way.'

'Indian country where we come from,' said Hope tersely. 'See the mules get fed well, won't you?'

'Best I got,' nodded the ostler. 'Your driver got a horse? Or does he . . .'

'I got a horse,' interrupted Azul. 'Needs a stall.'

For a moment the man looked as though he was going to argue, then he shrugged and said, 'Be two dollars fifty a day fer the horse. One fifty a head fer the mules. Wagon'll cost you three dollars a day.'

'That's twelve dollars a day for the wagon and team.' Grace made the calculation instantly. Fourteen fifty with the horse.'

Azul was still totting the figures, and it took the stablehand longer before he nodded. 'Yeah, that's right. You handle figures real good.'

'I should,' Grace said. 'I . . .'

'Grace! Let's not argue.' Hope climbed down from the seat unaided, her tone sharp, cutting off her daughter's sentence. 'The gentleman knows his own business. It's not for us to question him.'

She opened a bag as black as her dress, turning away as she counted out the notes. 'Here. Fourteen dollars and fifty cents. If we decide to stay longer, we'll pay you when we leave.'

'Fair enough, ma'am.' The man took the money and dropped it into his pocket, his pale eyes flitting from mother to daughter. 'Where's the horse?'

'I'll bring it round the front,' grunted Azul.

He climbed over the gate and picked up the reins of the grey stallion, walking the big horse back down the street to the front of the livery. The doors were open and as he went inside the ostler whistled appreciatively.

'That's one helluva pony you got there. Arab, ain't he?'

'Part,' Azul agreed. 'Rest's mustang.'

'Almighty fine horse fer a . . .' The man broke off when he turned from his admiration of the stallion and caught Azul's cold, blue stare. 'Fer a . . .'

'Halfbreed?' Azul supplied. 'Be a fine horse for anyone. An' in case you're thinking of fancy dealings, I got a bill on him. Gift from grateful friends.'

He omitted to say that the 'grateful friends' were both dead. In part as a result of his own actions: it was an episode in his life he preferred to forget.*

'Ain't doubting your word, mister,' said the limping man.

* *See BREED 9 – BLOOD-STOCK!*

'It's just unusual to see a feller like you mounted on so fine a pony.'

'Yeah.' Azul led the stallion into a stall, checking first that the straw was clean and the manger filled with decent fodder. After that he unbuckled the cinch and lifted the saddle clear of the grey's back. 'Rub him down, will you? An' treat him gentle.'

'Fifty cents extra fer a rub-down.' The stablehand's eyes got sly. 'Ain't included in the normal bill.'

Azul dug coins from his pocket and passed them over. 'Just do it right.'

'Sure. Sure will.'

The halfbreed dumped the saddle over the stall's gate, unfastening his bedroll and saddlebags and easing the Winchester clear of the scabbard. He slung the bags over his left shoulder and cradled the rifle in his left arm, pacing down the dim aisle to the rear door.

The two women were waiting for him by the side of the corral, deep in a conversation that ended abruptly as the rear door slammed shut. He walked over to them and opened the gate. They both carried small cases. Grace was looking around, her expression happier than Azul had ever seen it. It was as though she relished the idea of passing the night in a town so big as Santa Fe. Hope was frowning, glancing at her daughter and at Azul, then at the wagon.

'Will it be safe?' she asked. 'Do you trust him?'

Azul shrugged. 'Far as I trust anyone.'

'How far is that?' demanded the older woman.

As she spoke a soft, soggy squelching sound burst from one of the mules. The animal was defecating, its tail lifted high and its rump turned towards them. Flies swarmed about it. Azul grinned, pointing.

'About that far.'

The woman's face went pale, and beside her there was a gasp from her daughter.

'Everything we own is on that wagon.'

'So I'll save some money.' Azul shrugged, easing his

saddlebags down from his shoulder. 'I'll sleep in the wagon.'

The two women exchanged a swift glance, neither one seemed entirely happy with his suggestion, but Hope nodded. 'That's kind of you.'

Azul said nothing. Just went over to the wagon and dumped his gear inside. He laced the flaps of canvas covering front and rear together and rejoined the women.

'It should be safe until sundown. Let's find you a hotel.'

Half a block down there was a Spanish-style building with a name painted on the whitewash of the porch: Hotel Viridiana. It looked clean, the double doors opening on a glassed-in vestibule that, in turn, gave access to the lobby. The walls were white, decorated with Indian blankets and reproductions of famous paintings Azul had never seen. A flight of stairs led up to the first floor directly in front of the door; to the right was a bead-curtained room that smelt like the restaurant. To the left was a desk with a register, a bell-push, and a nameplate. The plate had the name *Ramon Bunuel* engraved on the brass. There was no one behind the desk, so Azul slapped the plunger of the bell.

A door opened and a short, middle-aged man stumbled out, trying hard to hurry while still pulling on a high, button-up boot. He looked vaguely embarrassed.

'*Buenas Dias.*' He got the boot on his foot and assumed a professional smile. 'You desire rooms?'

Azul glanced at Hope, who said, 'Just one. With a bath if you got it.'

The clerk looked at her. Then at Grace. Then at Azul.

Then, primly, he said: 'Most of our rooms are for one or two people, *madame*.' He emphasised the last word.

Grace blushed and turned away. Hope laughed.

'The room's for me and my daughter. Azul is sleeping elsewhere.'

'Azul?' He looked at the halfbreed. 'Kieron Gunn's boy?'

Azul nodded. 'You knew my father?'

'Knew him?' The Mexican smiled. 'Kieron helped me start this place. When he was trading out of Santa Fe he used to bring me shoes from the coast. A most discreet man. Very charming and not at all *bourgeois*. But what happened? I heard the exterminating angel claimed him.'

'He got killed by scalphunters,' rasped Azul; not wanting to remember. 'Along with my mother.'

'I am sorry.' The Mexican assumed a grave expression. 'Accept, please, the sincere regrets of Ramon Bunuel. In a land without bread men's minds often turn to murder.'

'Yeah,' grunted Azul. 'A man can get to be a brute.'

'The golden age is gone,' nodded Bunuel.

'I hate to break up this touching reunion,' said Hope Walls. 'But I'd like to clean up and get something to eat.'

'*Lo siento.*' Bunuel used the formal phrase. 'Your room shall be the best I can find for the companions of my old friend's son.'

He turned to select a key from the hooks backing the desk. Then took a second down.

'Both rooms are at the back, where it will be more quiet. One holds a double bed; the other, two smaller couches. They are separated by a bathroom.' He winked at Azul. 'I hope you will be happy there.'

'Give me the key to the singles,' said Hope. 'That'll suit us. He's not staying.'

Azul shrugged as Bunuel looked at him: 'I got a wagon to guard.'

'But you will eat here?' asked the Mexican hotel owner. 'On the house? In memory of your father.'

'Thanks.' Azul picked up the two cases, tucking the Winchester under his arm. 'Be honoured.'

'I shall order for you,' called Bunuel. 'The finest in the house.'

The room was cool and quiet, a window opening on to a street behind. There were glass panes and two heavy wooden shutters. The facing building was blank-walled, devoid of windows. Inside, there were two beds separated by a washstand, a set of pegs built into the side wall and a large wardrobe facing the beds to one side of the secondary door. Azul drew the bolt, opening the door on to a bathroom that boasted a regular supply of hot water from the intricate linkage of pipes and taps covering one wall before spreading over to the huge tub. He checked the facing door and found it locked, a bolt on the bathroom side affording privacy.

'Seems like they know you pretty well,' remarked Hope. 'I guess your father was a well remembered man.'

'He got around,' said Azul. 'He made friends.'

'But you don't.'

It was about the first comment Grace had addressed directly to the halfbreed.

'Not many, ma'am. I found out early that friends have a way of letting you down.' He paused, bolting the interior lock of the bathroom. 'At least white friends do.'

Grace gasped. 'I'm not taking that! I'm sorry, momma, but that is just too much!'

'You took worse,' said Hope. 'Shut up. We need him.'

'If you do,' said Azul, 'I'll be downstairs. In the restaurant.'

He picked up his rifle and left the room. Something prickled on his mind, allied to the doubts that had built up during the journey. It had to do with the way Grace dressed and the way her mother kept so close-mouthed about their destination; the worry over guarding the wagon; and the way the vehicle was so heavy.

He went down to the restaurant and let Bunuel pick him a table.

He ate a cold vegetable soup that he recalled was *gazpacho*; then a steak with fried potatoes and sweetcorn. He was drinking coffee when the two women entered the room. Hope Walls was wearing the same black dress as before, though now it was brushed clean of trail dirt, damp patches showing where she had scrubbed sweat marks away. Her daughter was dressed in green silk, the neck cut high, with a tiny frill of white silk accentuating her slender neck and finely-featured face.

He drank some brandy as the women began their meal and then excused himself, wandering out through the half-remembered streets.

He went inside the cathedral, but the priests there had all changed and he could not see one he knew from his past. Automatically, he checked the dodgers posted outside the sheriff's office, but saw no one that related to him.

He drank two whiskies in a saloon, thinking about the way Santa Fe had changed . . .

He remembered it best as a Spanish city: high white walls and sweet-smelling pine trees. Watching it from the cantle of his father's saddle as Kieron Gunn rode his pony across the plaza towards the cathedral. Rainbow Woman, his mother, had ridden a mustang alongside, and behind had come a column of Santa Fe traders and Apache warriors. Sees-The-Fox was there; and also Sees-Both-Ways; and many more Chiricahua, come to give their personal blessings to a ceremony alien to their own religion, but approved of because they held Kieron Gunn in such high regard.

He remembered the sour-smelling water sprinkled over his face. And the smiling face of the priest.

He remembered the celebration after, when his father and the Apaches and the traders had got drunk together. When there was a trade, and the land was not divided. And men felt no need to kill one another because it was easier to live in harmony . . .

He called for a third whisky to blot out the memories. Santa Fe was not a good place to visit: it held too many memories of times past and best forgotten, for they could never be regained.

It was late in the afternoon when he emerged from the saloon. The sun was lowering into the western horizon, sharding lances of brilliant light down the high-walled avenues, wreathing the spire of the cathedral in emberish red light.

His head was fugged by memories and alcohol so that he walked carefully, strolling along the sidewalks with exaggerated concentration. No one paid him much attention, the citizens too used to drunken drifters to worry overmuch about one more.

He paused outside the stable, then decided to go inside.

It was dark now that the afternoon was faded into evening, but a series of kerosene lanterns shed flickering light over the stalls. He checked the grey stallion: the horse had been rubbed down and seemed content in the stall, the straw still fresh and the manger still filled with fodder. A trough of fresh water stood to one side.

Outside, in the corral, the mules were chomping contentedly on the hay forked into the trough that lined the open-sided shed flanking the western wall. They had water and looked healthy. The wagon was still laced tight with no signs of entry.

He went back to the Viridiana.

'The two ladies are out still,' said Bunuel. 'I believe they went to buy clothes.'

'So I can take a bath,' said Azul. 'Lend me a towel?'

'A pleasure.' Bunuel disappeared into his office, emerging moments later with a huge fold of rough cotton. 'Here. No charge to the son of my friend.'

'Thanks.' Azul reached over to take the towel, noticing that the Mexican had changed his black, buttoned boots for a pair of black and white pumps. 'Thanks a lot.'

'*De nada.*' Bunuel passed the halfbreed a key. 'That will open the next room or the ladies' room.'

'Useful,' Azul grinned. 'Keep it well hid.'

'Don't worry, *amigo*. I do.'

Azul grinned and waved, striding up the staircase with a smile of anticipation on his face.

He knocked on the door of the women's room and got no answer. So he used the key, stepping straight through, after locking the door behind him, to the bathroom. He slid the bolt back and stepped inside. The farther door was still bolted shut, so he turned on the taps and watched the water spouting into the tub. Then he undressed and hung his clothes on the doorpegs. There was a wicker chair against the wall: he set his Colt on the seat after dragging the chair over to the side of the tub and then canted the Winchester against the back. Both guns stayed within easy reach.

The tub filled up and he climbed inside, luxuriating in the warmth that covered his body. He lay back, just letting the heat knead the trail stiffness from his limbs, keeping the plug out and the hot tap running. Then he picked up the bar of gritty soap that rested in a wire tray at the far end of the bath and began to scrub his body, starting at the top and working his way down. When he was finished he put the soap back and plugged the tub again, turning on the cold tap. The water made him shiver, but it washed the grime from his body and refreshed him at the same time, the alternation of hot and cold washing away the effects of the alcohol. He splashed around, then emptied the tub again before drenching himself in cold water.

Then he towelled dry and got dressed.

Before entering the room occupied by the two women he knocked on the door. There was no answer, so he unbolted the bathroom and stepped through. He went over to the main door and used Bunuel's key to open it. Stepping out into the corridor, he locked the door behind him and went back down the stairs.

'Thanks.' He passed the towel and the pass key to the Mexican. 'I appreciate that.'

'The least I could do.' Bunuel smiled. 'Given the understanding of your father.'

Azul glanced up at the clock set above the vestibule. It was close on six-thirty. 'You serving dinner yet?'

'For you, *mi amigo*, of course.'

The owner of the hotel escorted him through to the restaurant. Chose a table and called for service.

'Whatever he wants. It is on the house.'

Azul grinned and sat back in his chair, enjoying the unusual luxury. A waitress, no more than eighteen years old, and just approaching the full blooming of her Latin prettiness, came to take his order. He asked her what was best on the menu, and accepted her suggestions of corn on the cob followed by venison with cabbage and fries, then pumpkin pie. He refused any wine in favour of a pot of coffee, then watched the gradual trickle of diners enter the room. Most of them cast furious glances in his direction, and the aftermath of the liquor he had swallowed allowed him to be amused rather than angry.

The Viridiana was obviously a successful hotel, for most of the guests were dressed expensively, their well-cut clothes contrasting with the travel-stained gear of the halfbreed. In addition, few of the men were armed – only three wearing gunbelts, and two more showing the bulges of shoulder holsters beneath their coats – unlike the blond-maned man with the Colt on his hip and the Winchester propped against the wall beside his seat.

Adding to their curiosity was the fact that the hotel's owner came at regular intervals to speak with the halfbreed, making no attempt to hide his pleasure at Azul's presence.

By the time Hope and Grace Walls entered the room, Azul had explained the circumstances of his parents' death to Bunuel and told the Mexican of his job escorting the two women north. Bunuel hurried to seat them at Azul's table; though Grace looked annoyed at the placement, Hope appeared pleased to discuss their day.

'We got more maps,' she announced. 'In between my daughter picking up new dresses. They're Government Survey things, so they should be reliable. I reckon we need to skirt east of the Rockies as far as Trinidad, then we can follow the cattle trail up to Pueblo and Denver. Head on to Cheyenne and then pick up the Bozeman Trail to the Montana border. How's that sound to you?'

'Fine as far as Trinidad,' said Azul. 'Beyond that I don't know. I've never been that way. Like I told you. But Government maps should be as good as most, so they're most likely reliable.'

'I aim to leave in the morning,' said Hope. 'I don't want to stay around here too long.'

Azul shrugged. 'You're the boss.'

Grace said, 'Momma! We could rest over a few days. It wouldn't hurt any.'

The older woman concentrated on her soup. Then, 'You know we have to reach Jericho as fast as we can. Joshua's on his own up there since Ruth died. He needs family around. Besides he offered us a home, we got your daddy's papers to deliver. You forget towns for a spell and make a new life up north.'

'Momma!' Grace held her voice down to a whisper almost too low for Azul to hear. 'We could stay over.'

'Grace!' Hope Walls whispered too, but her voice cut angrily across her daughter's complaints. 'We got somewhere to go. A home. Don't argue about it.'

Azul decided it was time to back out from a family quarrel. He had finished his meal and could sense that the women were about to start another argument. He drank the last of his coffee and pushed his chair back.

'Forgive me, ladies, but I think it's time I checked the wagon again. If you want me I'll be inside.'

'He'll go off drinking,' Grace whispered to her mother. 'It won't be safe at all.'

'Close your mouth, girl!' Hope's voice got angry. 'I trust him.'

Azul smiled, standing up to cradle the Winchester in his arms.

'It's the last supper at the Viridinia, Grace, and all I want is sleep. I'll take that in the wagon. I promise I won't even touch your shoes.' He bowed cynically. 'If you want me, you know where to find me.'

The streets were partially lit by the kerosene lanterns hung from trees and saloons and the more regular poles erected by the City Council. Azul, more accustomed to moving through sunlight or shadow, felt oddly exposed by the permanent light of the flaring torches that danced inside the glassed-in containers.

He reached the stable and pushed through the side-door that flanked the main entrance.

There was no one inside; and that worried him. He checked the grey stallion and then the mules and the wagon. Nothing had happened.

He went back into the stable.

The limping man was seated inside the front entrance, spooning a mess of Chinese food up to his mouth. He jumped when Azul touched his shoulder, losing bean sprouts over his knees and choking on the ones gasped down his throat.

Azul feigned drunkenness.

'Want a place to sleep. Can't get a goddam hotel. Got some straw?'

The grey-haired man pointed at the loft.

'Can you make it up there? It'll cost you fifty cents.'

Azul let his rifle fall to the floor as he fumbled coins from his pocket.

'Count 'em for me, *amigo*. Then point me the direction. *Muy gracias*.'

The pinch-faced man took sixty cents and thumbed his hand at the ladder going up to the loft. 'I ain't hired to shove halfbreeds to bed. You bastards should learn to hold your likker.'

'Yeah.' Azul laughed. 'That's right. Hope I don't fall on you.'

He climbed the ladder. Behind him he could hear the stablehand mumbling about drunken *injuns* and how crossbreeding was the worst.

He got up into the straw bales stacked along both sides of the storage walls built out above the central aisle. At front and back they were open to the loading windows that gave access to the street and corral.

Both openings had pulleys built out from the walls, the

ropes coiled neatly on the small platforms. Azul checked the rope at the rear, deciding that it was strong enough to support his weight, then moved silently back along the loft. He stretched out with the Winchester in his hands and feigned a drunken snore.

Below, he could hear the ostler slurping up the last of his Chinese dinner. A burp, followed by the clatter of plates. Azul snored again.

'Hey! Halfbreed! You awake?'

He ignored the shout, listening to the limping man as he shuffled along the aisle to the rear door. The bolt scraped back and the man whistled into the night. Azul crawled back to the loading window in time to see three shadows clamber over the fence and cross the corral. He eased back as they approached the stable.

'Anyone about?'

The voice was harsh; not one he recognised. The next was familiar: it belonged to the stablehand.

'The halfbreed's in the loft. Sleeping off a drunk, I'd reckon.'

'Best be sure,' came the grating answer. 'Ben, you climb up there an' kill him. The rest of us'll check the wagon over.'

The rear door slammed shut as boots thudded on the rungs of the ladder. Azul wriggled snake-like to the edge of the loft, drawing the Bowie knife as the would-be killer clambered upwards.

The halfbreed could hear the man's breath coming in short gasps as he climbed, and guessed him to be overweight. He was grumbling softly so that Azul could tell easily how high he was up the ladder. Azul grinned, anticipating the moment when the man's head would appear over the rim of the loft.

'Going up in the world,' he murmured to himself. 'But for where you're headed, that's the wrong direction.'

A pudgy hand with blackened nails chewed down to the quick showed at the ladder's head. Then a sweat-stained brown hat tilted back from a moon face. The right hand appeared, clutching a long Green River knife.

'Go to hell,' Azul snarled.

And lunged forwards.

Chapter Four

Ben looked to weigh in excess of two hundred pounds, most of it distributed around his waist and jaw. He was sweating profusely – from the exertion of the climb rather than from fear, for his small, brown eyes were hard and cold, and he tried to bring the long-bladed knife into play as he spotted Azul's movement.

The halfbreed was advantaged by his position and his natural speed. The Bowie flashed past the Green River knife to imbed its tip in the underfolds of Ben's multiple chins.

Azul halted the thrust so that the point remained in the flesh without severing anything vital. He smiled: 'Keep on coming. Without the knife.'

Ben looked into the cold, blue eyes and let go the hilt of his own weapon. A trickle of blood ran down beneath his open collar. His sweat got thicker, giving off a rank smell as he climbed on to the platform. Azul rose to his feet, still holding the Bowie under the man's jaw.

'Why?' he asked.

'Jesus Christ! I don't know!' Ben was getting frightened now. 'Al told me to kill you, that's all.'

'And you do what Al tells you?' said Azul. 'No questions asked.'

He used the knife as a goad, driving Ben round until the fat man was backed up against a pile of hay bales, then reached forwards with his left hand to lift the Colt from Ben's holster. He tossed the pistol aside.

'Who is Al?'

'Al Bennet. I'm Ben Marsh. The other one is Vic Strother.' The words came in a rush as his initial determination evaporated into naked terror. 'Al's the boss. We just go along.'

He was wearing a thick plaid shirt against the night's chill, but now the material seemed to soften and thin out as fear sweat burst from his pores. Azul turned the knife, setting the cutting edge against Ben's windpipe.

'What are they looking for?'

'I don't know!' The voice assumed a whining quality. 'Al looks after that side o' things.'

'So you're just muscle that doesn't know what's going on?'

'That's right.' Ben would have nodded had the movement not threatened to kill him. 'Al has some kinda deal goin'. We got a hundred apiece to watch fer a wagon with two women . . . Never thought to find you. Leastways, not until Charlie told us.'

'Charlie?' Azul leant slightly forwards, pressing the blade deeper into the trembling flesh. 'Who's he?'

'Stableman. Feller with the limp. Al promised him twenty dollars fer word. Same as he promised all the others. That's all I know, mister. Honest.'

'I believe you,' grunted Azul, meaning it: Ben was far too frightened to hold anything back. 'Trouble is, it don't do you any good.'

'What you mean?' Fresh runnels of sweat coursed down Ben's cheeks. 'I told you everything I know.'

'Exactly,' said Azul.

And slashed the Bowie across the fat man's throat.

Between two of Ben's chins lips of red appeared, spurting sudden fountains of crimson. The overweight killer gasped, then lifted his hands to his neck as he realised that his breath was leaking out through the cut. Azul stepped to the side as the blood gouted across the loft. Ben tried to scream, but when he opened his mouth only a faint, shrill whistling sound came out. His face went pale as his hands got dark with blood. He fell down on his knees, eyes wide and staring as the knowledge of his death imprinted on his mind.

Azul brought his arm down in a curving arc, driving the

Bowie knife deep into the back of Ben's neck. The tip appeared for a moment between the man's fingers, then withdrew as the halfbreed twisted the blade and dragged it clear. Now crimson gushed from both sides of the throat, soaking into the stacked hay so that the dry fodder crackled and sighed, as though grateful for the ghastly watering.

Ben collapsed on to his face, his body heaving as fear choked vomit up his windpipe to join the blood already draining from his body. He was dead before Azul reached the Winchester, his stained hands clutching uselessly at the straw as the final vestiges of his life ran out through the cuts and began to drip on to the floor below.

Azul lifted the rifle and worked the action to slide a shell into the firing chamber. Then he went to the loading platform at the rear of the stable and picked up the rope. Below him he could see the stablehand limping nervously around the wagon as the two other men rummaged amongst the interior contents. He ran the rope back inside, looping one end around Ben's ankles, fastening the other to the stanchion inside the window. He dragged the corpse along the loft, then shoved it clear, listening to the hiss of the unspooling rope as he slid down the ladder and ran for the door.

'Ben? Quit foolin' about, you goddam idiot.'

He recognised Charlie's voice as he eased out into the corral, then heard a sudden intake of breath as the crippled man realised that it was not him, but Ben, dangling on the end of the rope.

'Al? Fer Chrissakes, Al!'

The warning ended abruptly as the halfbreed crossed the yard and brought his Winchester round in a short, vicious arc that began at his shoulder and ended at Charlie's jaw. He was holding the rifle in both hands, the left clutching the barrel, the right hooked into the trigger and lever. His left acted as pivot, his right as driving force: the point of the stock hit the ostler on the curve of his jaw, just where the bone was jointed to the upper part of the skull. Charlie's mouth snapped shut and his knees folded. He was still going down as Azul swung the rifle back and up, this time landing the flat of the stock against the underside of the jaw. Charlie's head jerked back with a soggy sound and his head flopped to one side, blood trickling from his mouth and nostrils.

Azul let him fall, realising that the two blows had broken the man's neck. He hadn't really planned it that way, but found it impossible to feel any regret: Charlie had set him up for a killing and was now reaping the unexpected reward of his betrayal. Azul moved towards the wagon.

The men inside were too intent on their search to have heard the faint sounds outside. Azul could see them shadowed against the canvas as a lantern burned, outlining their bodies like the figures in a shadow play.

He cocked the Winchester and stepped up to the tail-gate.

'You find what you're looking for?'

One man was tall and thin, dressed all in black, with a pair of matched Smith & Wesson Americans tied down on his thighs. He looked to be about forty years old, with a hollow face fixed in a permanent sneer. His companion was younger by a good twenty years, dressed in worn Levis and a dark blue shirt. He carried a Colt on his left hip, butt-forwards, cross-draw fashion.

Both men looked up, but it was the younger who reached for his gun.

Azul's bullet took him in the throat, opening a hole through his neck that emitted very little blood until the slug exited from the back. It tore a hole in the canvas that was rapidly covered with the thick fountaining of crimson gouting behind the lead. The man – Azul guessed he was Vic Strother – pitched backwards against the stain of his own life. The canvas, laced to the curving ribs of the conestoga's roof, acted as a kind of trampoline, bouncing the choking thief off in a springy dive that pitched him clear over the tailgate.

Azul ducked aside, lifting the reloaded Winchester to cover the last man.

Strother rested on his side. His Colt was in his hand, but the thumb and forefinger were no longer capable of working the action. Gurgling sounds came from his mouth and the holes in his neck; his eyes remained wide open, staring up at the halfbreed even as they dimmed and clouded over.

The man in black stood up, dropping the box he had been holding.

'You kill them all?'

Azul nodded. 'I reckon.' He glanced down at Strother. The eyes were still open, but now they were milky. Blank. Something like a cough echoed deep inside the young gunman and his feet drummed against the ground. Then he stiffened. 'Yeah,' Azul said.

'Then maybe we can deal. I'm Al Bennett.'

Azul kept the Winchester pointed at the thin man. 'I figgered that. Ben Marsh said you were the boss.'

Bennett chuckled. 'There could be a thousand in it. But decide fast, on account of there's folks comin' to check the shooting.'

Azul heard shouts from the entrance of the street, followed by the stamping of feet.

'All right,' he said. 'Move out. Fast.'

There was no point in staying around while a bunch of white citizens discovered three bodies: the outcome was too predictable. Three dead white men and a halfbreed with a bloodied knife and still-smoking rifle added up to a lynching party or a long spell in jail. The scene had been played out too many times before, and if the approaching citizens found him there with Al Bennett, it would be Bennett whose word was believed, and Azul's body that hung from the gallows.

He followed the black-clad man over the farther fence as the first of the citizens rushed into the corral.

The fence shut the stable off from a garbage-littered backlot and a tall, empty office building. Screeching cats ran from the mess as the two men raced through the filth covering the ground. Bennett jumped on to a metal bin to facilitate his climb over the far wall. Azul matched the thin man's speed by tossing his rifle into the alley beyond and taking the wall at a run. He sprang upwards, fastening both hands over the rim and using his momentum to power up and astride the bricks.

He rolled clear, landing in the alley and picking up his Winchester while Bennett was still easing gingerly over the rough stones.

Then he followed the gunman north into the redlight district. Bennett halted, panting, a block down from a big house with a kerosene lantern flanked by a line of drying stockings.

Azul cocked the Winchester: 'Unload the pistols.'

'Hell!' Bennett was a shadow against the faint light. 'I thought we had ourselves a deal.'

'I hold the ace.' Azul brought the rifle up to his shoulder. 'And now I'm seeing you.'

'Jesus!' complained Bennett. 'Don't you trust anyone?'

Azul just laughed and began to take up the trigger slack.

Bennett lifted his guns out from the holsters. He was good. It showed in the way he thumbed the latches clear of the cylinders so that both pistols ejected their loads together. The brass shells danced over the dry ground, spraying like deadly confetti around Bennett's feet.

'They cost money,' he complained. 'You want me to leave them there?'

'Man with a thousand dollars to spend can afford new bullets,' Azul rasped. 'Where we going?'

Bennett shrugged and holstered the empty guns. 'In there.'

There was the cathouse up the block, its porch guarded by a massive negro dressed in red livery and cradling a pick shaft in his arms. The upper end of the wooden stave was wrapped in leather, through which protruded the points of thick nails.

He stood aside as Bennett went in, followed closely by Azul. He was several inches taller than the halfbreed, and as he turned to open the doors his white-powdered wig caught its tail on the frame and twisted the whole thing clear to expose the crinkly black hair underneath the white falseness.

Azul grinned and followed Bennett inside.

The exterior door opened on a wide vestibule with coats hung along one side. A shelf supported about thirty hats, ranging from stetsons to derbys. Beyond there was another door, allowing entry to a room filled up with women and dancing men. The women were dressed in garter belts and stockings, or flimsy dresses or dark lace that hid little of their bodies. Their expressions were uniform with boredom.

Off to one side there was a cork-fronted bar. Behind which a fat lady spread her weight over a chair. She looked up as Bennett came in.

The hired killer smiled and pointed at the stairs leading up to the first floor. Azul smiled, canting the Winchester on his shoulder as he paced the gunman up the stairs.

Bennett's room was on the first storey, facing out to the alley. It was small: a bed and wash-stand taking up most of the room. There was a window with drawn blinds and a cupboard that held one single black stormcoat and a Browning shotgun.

Azul checked the ugly-looking scattergun, dragging the shells out while Bennett locked the door.

'Christ!' The dark man settled himself on the bed. 'I thought you were gonna kill me. I saw that goddam rifle pointed my way and reckoned it was the end. You know the feeling? When you think everything's coming to a full stop?'

Azul nodded. 'I felt it.'

'Jesus!' Bennett went on nodding. 'I'm glad you was willing to listen to reason. Makes sense to make a deal. Right?'

'Right,' answered Azul. 'But the right depends on the deal. So tell me about this one.'

Bennett looked at the muzzle of the Winchester and began

to sweat like Ben Marsh.

'I don't know much about it.' He backed down the bed, followed by Azul's rifle. 'I got word that a man in Wyoming wanted the women stopped. Didn't matter how, just so long as it got done. He was ready to pay three thousand dollars.'

'That's too much money for stopping a wagon.' Azul shoved the rifle tight against Bennett's chin. 'What's the payload?'

'Christ! I don't know. All I got was this letter.'

Bennett reached inside his coat, fumbling around in search of the missing document.

Then his hand lifted clear with a Remington derringer blasting fire into Azul's face.

The outflash of the ·41 calibre blinded Azul as he powered clear of the bed. He felt the *whirr* of the bullet. And squeezed the trigger of his own gun in automatic retaliation.

The Winchester blasted a hole through Al Bennett's chest. It landed its ·44-40 slug in the wall behind, matching the mess Vic Strother had left inside the wagon. Azul triggered again, still blinded, sighting and firing on pure instinct.

He hit Bennett twice more in the chest and once in the face.

The killer's shirt got bright with spilling blood as the slugs pumped through his body. The derringer blasted its last slug into the ceiling, producing a scream from the room above.

Azul glanced at the window and jammed the cupboard against the door. The cupboard was built thin, but still hard enough to hold the entrance for a few minutes. He opened the window and smashed the blinds outwards. Below him there was a narrow porch. As hands began to thump against the door he powered through the window frame, landing on the roof of the porch on his left shoulder. Tiles shifted under his weight, and he felt himself sliding clear.

A gun barked, blasting flame through the night. He rolled,

slipping down into the alley below in a welter of skidding slates.

He ducked back under the overhang as the gun flamed again. Then he sidled down the porch and began to run to the join of two adjacent alleys.

The gun echoed flame three more times, but by now he was confident that the shots were for show, rather than aimed at a clear target. He ducked into the alley and slowed his pace to a walk, emerging on the western edge of main street as a crowd began to gather around the walls of the stable.

He walked slowly back to the Hotel Viridiana, meeting Hope and Grace Walls inside the vestibule.

'What's happening?' they asked in unison. 'Everyone got woken by the fight in the stable.'

'The wagon's safe.' Azul steered them towards the stairs. 'But I'm not. I need an alibi.'

'What happened?' Hope locked the door of their room and motioned Azul to a chair.

'The stablehand passed word on to three gunmen.' The halfbreed looked hard at the grey-haired woman. 'Seems like they were expecting you. Someone offered three thousand dollars to stop you reaching Wyoming.'

'And they were in the wagon?' asked Hope, cautiously. 'You surprised them?'

Azul nodded.

'Did you kill them?' It was Grace who spoke now. 'All of them?'

Azul could not tell if her eyes were lit up with concern or vicarious excitement. He nodded again, 'Yeah. I killed them.'

'Did they find anything?' Now it was Hope again, her voice wary. 'Did you see?'

'No to both questions.' Azul shook his head, then: 'I think it's time I knew what's so special about that wagon. There's six men dead from trying to stop you, and I could get posted in Santa Fe.'

'You said there were only three thieves.' Again Grace

demonstrated her skill with figures. 'Three and the two back south makes five.'

'The stablehand was there.' Azul spread the fingers of one hand out, then lifted the middle finger of the other. 'He made six.'

He stood up and went over to the bathroom door. There was no sound from the inside, so he opened the door and crossed to the tub. The cold tap sluiced Ben Marsh's blood from the knife, and Azul dried it on a towel. He went back to the women's room and bolted the door. Hope and Grace were staring at one another like two people frozen in the middle of an argument.

'Well?' Azul demanded. 'Do you tell me? Or do I quit?'

It was Grace who answered, her voice hard. 'If you quit now, we'll tell the marshal it was you who killed those men.'

'You do that,' Azul said softly, his voice cold, 'an' I'll tell him why. Chances are he'll impound your wagon and hold you as witnesses.'

Grace's face went pale, then flushed with anger. She opened her mouth to speak again, but her mother hushed her.

'I think we have to tell him now,' she said. 'We've come too far together.'

Grace shrugged. 'As you like, momma.'

'When we left Mexico,' said the older woman, 'we brought with us a number of documents relating to our possessions there. We own a number of profitable land deeds, not least those covering the mine. They would be worth a great deal of money to anyone able to prove they had title. Not all of our relations are as honest as my brother.'

'So it could be a family affair,' Azul said. 'Someone related to you might be trying to cash in?'

'That's the only thing I can think of,' replied Hope. 'I don't know who, but only our immediate family could possibly know about the deeds.'

'Or where you're heading,' said Azul. 'And which route you'd take.'

Hope nodded, her eyes sad. Azul glanced at Grace: the younger woman was expressionless, her face blank as a mask. Azul shrugged.

'Best push on, then. But meanwhile, we need to agree a story.'

'What about?' asked Hope.

'Where I've been tonight,' said the halfbreed. 'Before long someone is going to connect that wagon to you, and find out where you're staying. They'll want to know why there are three dead men around it.'

'You said you killed four,' interrupted Grace.

'I killed the last one in a cathouse.' Azul wondered why the woman's face lit up. 'At least two people saw me going in.'

Grace laughed softly. 'So you need us as much as we need you.'

'I guess so,' he acknowledged.

A fist hammered against the door.

'What shall we say?' whispered Hope.

'Ask them to wait,' murmured Azul. 'Grace! You got those maps?'

The dark-haired woman nodded and fetched the surveys from the wardrobe, suddenly in tune with Azul's demands. She spread them over one of the beds as her mother called out that she was coming to the door. Azul shifted across, seating himself beside Grace so that it looked like they were both studying the maps.

Hope opened the door.

The marshal was about six and a half feet tall, wearing a dark brown broadcloth suit with the jacket hiked back over the butt of the Remington Army model holstered high on his waist so that the brass star pinned to his vest was clearly visible. His hair and moustache matched the colour of the suit and the walnut stock of the Browning shotgun he carried. His eyes were grey. And suspicious.

'Ma'am.' He touched his left hand to the brim of his brown

stetson. The right went on pointing the scattergun into the room. 'Can I come in a moment?'

'I guess.' Hope Walls stood back: an old, nervous lady, anxious to help the law. 'I was just going over our journey with my daughter and our guide.'

Azul admired her control. He had to: it was superb.

The marshal stepped inside.

'Parton,' he said. 'Marshal John Parton.' He looked at Hope. 'You'd be Mrs Walls?'

'I am.' She ducked a curtsey, then gestured at Grace and Azul. 'And this is my daughter, Grace. And our guide, Mr Gunn.'

'Gunn?' Parton frowned. 'I heard that name before.'

'My pa was a Santa Fe trader,' said Azul. 'I got christened in the cathedral. You might have heard the name that way.'

He hoped Parton hadn't seen it on a dodger.

'You heard what happened?' The marshal addressed the question to the room in general. 'About the killings?'

'We heard there was a fight down by the stable,' said Azul. 'That's all.'

Parton frowned. 'How come you didn't go check?'

Hope Walls stepped in fast: 'We thought you'd have it under control, Marshal Parton. Mr Gunn wanted to check, but we insisted he stay here. We felt sure you'd want to talk with us, and it seemed the wisest course to stay where you could find us easily.'

'An' you all been here together?' queried Parton. 'All evenin'?'

'Most of it,' said Hope. 'Mr Gunn went for a stroll earlier, but that was long before the trouble started. My daughter and I can vouch for that.'

Parton nodded. 'Yes, ma'am. You know how many men were killed?'

'No.' Hope assumed a blank expression. 'I just heard there was some kind of fight.'

'Charlie Martin got his neck broke,' said Parton. 'He was

the owner of the stable. Feller with a limp – got his leg messed up in the Civil War. The others were drifters. One had his throat slit an' the others got shot. One right inside your wagon.'

'Perhaps Mr Martin was defending our property,' said Hope Walls; primly. 'He promised us a full-time guard.'

'He wasn't armed,' grunted Parton. 'Fact is that one feller got cut up with a knife an' the others were killed with a gun. Rifle, by my guess.'

'Dear me.' Hope swung easily into the part of a worried old lady. 'How awful. Thank God we're leaving in the morning.'

Marshal Parton looked at Azul: 'The last one was shot in a brothel.'

'Marshal!' Hope flustered like a broody hen. 'Please!'

'Sorry, ma'am.' Parton got confused. 'Fact is that the man on the door an' the lady inside gave a fair description of your guide there.'

'But Mr Gunn has been with us since before the trouble began,' lied Hope. 'My daughter will bear that fact out. Who would you sooner believe, marshal? The kind of people who run a . . . Well, a *house*, shall we say? Or three respectable travellers?'

She looked up at the lawman, somehow hunching her shoulders so that she resembled nothing so much as a tiny, worried mother, defending her brood. The lawman shrugged and looked away.

'I guess I have to believe you, ma'am.'

'I should hope so. Why, the very thought is horrifying! Mr Gunn has proved a most capable guide. I am sure he would have nothing to do with such brutal murders.'

'No, ma'am. But . . .'

'You said one of them was killed inside the wagon.' Hope interrupted. 'I presume that means they were trying to rob us. I trust you have placed a guard there?'

Parton swallowed hard. 'Got two deputies, ma'am. Both posted at the stable. Your wagon's safe until the morning.'

'Good, good.' Hope patted the marshal's arm. 'Thank you, Mr . . . ?'

'Parton, ma'am.'

'Parton . . . Yes, thank you, Mr Parton. Now if you'll forgive us, we must decide on our future route.'

'You'll be leaving in the morning?' said the marshal. 'Like you said?'

'I told you that,' frowned Hope. 'Or do you plan to arrest me?'

'No, ma'am. I got no grounds.' The tall peace officer backed out through the door. 'Sorry to have disturbed you, ma'am.'

'That's all right, Mr . . . ?'

'Parton.'

'Yes. Of course I'll forgive you.'

'No, ma'am. I said *Parton.*'

'Quite.'

Hope closed the door.

Chapter Five

Parton watched them go. It was soon after sun-up, the sky clear of clouds and a pale yellow orb climbing steadily across the eastern horizon. The air was cool, but the day promised to be bright and clear once the morning mist had lifted.

Hope handled the team and Azul rode the grey stallion alongside the wagon. The peace officer waved to him as they went by, indicating that the halfbreed should stop.

Azul turned the part-Arab, reining in alongside the marshal.

'Don't come back,' said Parton. 'Not while I'm peace officer here.'

Azul grinned. 'You're the boss.'

'No.' Parton shook his head. 'That little old lady's the boss. But next time you might not have her to protect you.'

They moved out from Santa Fe, heading northwards along the line of the Rio Grande in the direction of Taos. It was the easiest route; in fact, the only viable one short of the long swing east of the hills along the line of the railroad. But that would have meant a detour of at least two days, whereas the river route, albeit hard, was faster.

And both the women expressed a desire for speed.

In turn, Azul was glad to ride clear of the possibility of another spell in jail. Parton's suspicion was obvious and while the halfbreed remained curious as to the exact nature of the women's journey, he was equally anxious to avoid the chance of confinement.

They moved slowly along the valley cut by the river, their

path flanked by mountains on both sides. Azul kept watch, scouting the trail ahead and then riding back past the wagon to check their rear.

He remained curious about the exact nature of the journey, but was determined to bring them through to Jericho. There, he thought, the answer might emerge. There, the face of the man – or woman? – who was attempting to stop them might become visible. And meanwhile, there was nothing to do but push on.

It took five days to reach Taos, each one starting at dawn and ending only when the sun went down behind the Rockies and left the trail in darkness. They purchased fresh supplies there and passed the night in a pair of rooms built out behind a stinking saloon. The beds were bug-ridden and the next day they halted at noon to wash the bites in a cool stream that flowed down from the Moro Peaks.

Nine days later they crossed the pass leading to Trinidad.

The stone lifted up on either side: a massive, rocky spine that cut the eastern side of the country off from the western territories. The sheer faces of the cliffs lifted up thousands of feet above them, thick with pine trees and the remnants of winter's snow. It was cooler here, the last breaths of winter still lingering amongst the shadowed ravines, the walls of rock blocking out the sun so that they moved often in a kind of half-light. Azul supplemented their bought food with fresh meat: deer and bighorn sheep that he hunted and killed, regretting the fact that he had no time to use the whole of the dead animals as his mother's people would have done. Instead, he simply shot as much meat as they needed; butchered it, and then left the hides and bones behind, taking only the meat. Had he been alone – or moving with a group of Indians – he would have waited to flay the hides, preparing them for use as clothing or tent-making materials. The sinews and the bones would have been treated to provide cords for bows, glue for the lodges, weapons; all that a band of Indians needed. The bones would have made flensing tools; been layered into lengths stuck together with the glue of the marrow and the binding of the tendons to create the powerful bows favoured by the Apache and the Plains Indians alike. The hills were rich with shards of flint that could have been chipped down to make heads for the arrows that would be fashioned from the sprouting limbs of the trees. And the partridges, eagles and buzzards that constantly followed their path would have provided feathers for the flights. The sheepskins would have made warm clothing; the deerhides, useful moccasins, or leggings, or waterproof tents. Nothing would have been wasted.

But Azul was travelling the white man's road, and so all these things were left behind, to be found and used, or to rot away. Like the bones of the buffalo after the hunters had taken the meat to ship East. Leaving behind only the stench of death and the lonely monuments of wind-scoured whiteness.

They reached Trinidad and spent two days there, resting the mules and Azul's stallion before pressing on to join the path of the Goodnight-Loving cattle trail that began in Fort Concho, in Texas, and curved up through New Mexico and Colorado as far as Pueblo.

At this time of year, the trail was empty. The big drives would not start until the weather was warmer and the grass along the way thick enough to support the thousands of cows that were driven regularly to market.

They made good time, the going ahead eased by the pounding hoofs that had gone before. Winter was beginning to turn into spring, and the bulk of the Great Divide sheltered them from the winds that blew down from the north.

They crossed the line of the Atchison, Topeka and Santa Fe railroad at a place with no name. There was just a group of houses huddling against the flat of the prairie like old women hunching under their shawls to hide from the chill. There were six shacks, one of them a saloon and the rest dwelling places. There was a water pump feeding the railroad and a wide cattle trough, the ground around deepened by the hoofs so that a massive circle of indented ground – like a moat – surrounded the catch tank. The rails were shored up with wood where the cows had stamped the ground down. The wagon bounced and rattled over the metal lines.

They spoke little along the way, Azul preferring to leave the initiative to the women – which meant that he spoke mostly with Hope. Grace remained withdrawn, acknowledging the halfbreed only as a hired hand; ignoring her mother's admonitions to express more friendliness towards their guide and guard.

Three days north of the railroad Azul picked up Indian signs.

At first it was just old pony tracks, but as they moved farther north he saw fresher spoor. Droppings that were not yet solidified by sun and wind; the occasional ashes of a dead fire; discarded arrow heads.

On the fourth day he saw them.

The wagon was moving slowly down a wide valley, the sides so shallow that the wind, having shifted round to the east, blew clear and clean over the rim. They were dressed in hide leggings and beaded shirts, buffalo skin cloaks wrapped about their shoulders. Their hair was long, either braided into plaits or left loose to flutter about their faces. They wore eagle feathers in their hair, the tips stained with red and black dye. Three carried rifles; three more, bone bows; the others, lances and hide-covered shields.

They made no attempt to approach the wagon, just watched its progress along the valley the same way vultures watch a flagging animal: waiting for the right moment.

Azul reined in, allowing the wagon to draw level. Hope was handling the team with all the skill of an experienced mule skinner, and Grace was looking bored, a Winchester propped carelessly against the seat beside her. Neither woman seemed to have noticed the Indians; Hope because she was intent on the mules and Grace because nothing along the trail interested her. It was only the prospect of staying over in a town that brought any animation to her lovely face. Azul made a fast calculation: the mules had been plugging steadily onwards since just after sun-up, and now it was close on noon. The animals were strong, sturdy enough to keep the wagon moving all day if necessary without a break, but they would never succeed in out-running the fleet mustangs of the strange Indians. He wondered if either woman could handle a gun: if the watchers attacked, three rapid-firing Winchesters would outgun them; but that advantage depended on Hope and Grace knowing how to use a carbine effectively.

'Don't look now.' He kept his voice casual, as though remarking on some curiosity of the landscape. 'But we got company.'

Grace reached automatically for the carbine, her green eyes lifting to scan the terrain. She saw the Indians and gasped.

Azul snapped, 'Don't touch the gun! They're just watching us so far. Maybe they'll let us through. Keep moving, an' don't pay them much attention.'

Hope nodded her agreement. 'He's right, honey. I heard tell that sometimes these injuns will just let a traveller pass by.'

'He should know,' snapped Grace, but her hand came away from the carbine. 'He's one of them, after all.'

'No,' said Azul, 'I'm not. I never saw Indians like that before. We're too far north for Apache or Comanche, so these must be Plains Indians.'

He paced the wagon, keeping most of his attention fixed on the horsemen who had now lined themselves along the ridge to the west. He racked his brain to delve up a half-forgotten conversation with his father.

They had been riding together to Trinidad, where an old friend of Kieron Gunn's had a wagonload of carbines and cartridges he was prepared to sell to his late trapping partner. Kieron had agreed to negotiate the deal on behalf of the *rancheria*, knowing that the weapons would afford the Chiricahua both defence against the increasing spread of land-hungry white men and a good chance to kill more game to stock against the winter. The trader had two strange Indians with him. Azul could not understand their language, though his father had a few words. He had been impressed by them: they were taller than the Chiricahua, long, lean men with dark hair strung through with beads and coloured quills. They carried buffalo hide shields and tall lances, decorated with feathers. One of them had worn a quill shirt, the spines woven together so that twin sections covered his chest and back. The quills were laced together under his arms, covered with symbols in red and black and green.

'*They're Cheyenne*,' Kieron Gunn had explained later. '*They live on the Plains. Mostly north of the Arkansas river. Your mother's folk ain't the only Indians, boy. There's Comanche and Kiowa out on the Texas flatlands, an' a whole lot more all over this country. Hell! They owned it once. Before us white men came along to take it off them. The Cheyenne are part of a big bunch that professors call the Lakota. Farther north there's a tribe called the Sioux, an' that's split into a mess of different groups. Just like the Chiricahua and the Jicarillo and the Mimbreño.*'

Azul had been little more than twelve then, and his vision of the world was mostly limited to the confines of his surroundings. He had realised that the different tribes of Apacheria were essentially of the same stock, divided by the places in which they chose to live. He had known that Comanches and Kiowas dwelt eastwards of the Apache country, where the land got flat and boring, empty of mountains. And that to the south there were Yaquis – who were almost the same as the Apache – but he had never thought that there might be anyone else.

'*It's the same with white men*,' his father had told him. '*My folks was from Scotland. But there's Irishmen and Welshmen an' Cornishmen. All different. Then there's black men an' the Chinee. I even heard there's people living way up north, where the land ain't nothing but snow and ice, called Esquimaux. Build houses out of the ice an' live off things called seals or whales. Something like that. Fact is, the world's filled up with different people. All colours. But everyone's got two legs an' two arms. An' all most people want is to enjoy bein' alive without worryin' all the time about who might take their land or their wife. It's the folk who always want more who make the troubles.'*

'But we fight the Comanche,' Azul had said. 'Sees-The-Fox told me that we raid their pony herds and then they chase us so we have to fight them.'

'*Yeah.*' Kieron Gunn had smiled then and run a hand through his hair, like a man tired. '*But not often. We do it because we want ponies. The Comanche raid us because they want women, or their ponies back. If we could work out a trade, like we're doing now, then we could settle those differences.*' His face had gotten gloomy then. '*If everyone traded like the old days, there wouldn't be no trouble.*'

But trouble was there. It came with every wagon train that crossed the Indian lands, frightening the buffalo and dropping settlers like a blight on the open country. It came with the towns and the railroads and the forts, each new aggression driving away the creatures that were life and warmth and hope to the Indians. Killing the animals that were food and clothing, weapons and homes; destroying the entire basis of Indian culture so that the first owners of the land – the first dwellers on it – had nothing left to do but fight. To fight for their lives against the overwhelming flood of white men who took the land and drove the buffalo away. Who opened mines in the ground, like pock marks on a blistered face, and paid no heed to the upset they caused, spreading their waste and bringing new influxes of settlers to the open, clean, country. Who criss-crossed the plains and the hills with iron rails, and built towns around each place where the locomotives – the iron horses – stopped, so that the animals went away and the Indians were left with nothing.

Except the bullets of the blue-coated soldiers who defended the rape of the land.

'Reckon they're probably Cheyenne,' he said, recalling the name. 'They might let us through.'

'Suppose they don't?' asked Hope. 'What then?'

'Can you handle a gun?' Azul replied. 'Either of you?'

'I can,' said Hope, firmly. 'Fought your kin down in Mexico. Bandits, too.'

'No.' Grace shook her head. 'I never fired a gun in my life.'

'So let's hope they don't attack,' grinned Azul. 'If they do, halt the wagon an' get inside. Use the walls for cover an' hit as many as you can.'

'Why not run for it?' asked Hope. 'They might give up.'

'They'd outpace us.' Azul shook his head. 'The mules can't race a mustang, an' all they need do is put one arrow into the leader.'

'Is that what you'd do?' asked Grace, tartly. 'Being used to this kind of thing.'

'Only sensible thing to do,' grunted the halfbreed. 'If they attack, they'll come from the front.' He glanced at the low walls of the valley. 'Most likely ride in head-on to drop the first two in the team before splitting off to the sides. If you stay on the seat, they'll just ride past an' spread out behind. Where you can't hit them. Then they'll pick us off when we stop moving.'

He looked at both the women, his voice getting hard and cold, emphasising the gutteral tones of his Apache childhood.

'If I shout, you set the brake. Then get inside the wagon, one to each side. And fire at anything that moves. Try to hit the ones with guns first, then the bowmen.'

'But if they kill the mules we can't go on,' complained Grace.

'They'll only kill one or two,' said Azul. 'As many as they need to stop us.'

'But if they all get killed . . .'

'Then we walk. If we're still alive.'

The women looked at one another, both frowning. Azul said, 'You'll be able to carry the papers.' But they went on frowning so that he went on wondering exactly what their mission entailed.

The wagon went on down the valley, moving slowly, not hurrying. The nine Cheyenne went on watching, sitting their ponies like unmoving statues, only their eyes shifting to follow the course of the big cart.

The valley opened out at its northernmost rim into a wide basin. Off to the west there were the edges of the Moro Peaks, the dark timber flanking the sides shining green and black in the afternoon sun. To the east, the land lifted in a gentle rise, disappearing in a series of folds that were beginning to show the first sproutings of the spring grass. Ahead, the country wound out over folds and ridges that were intercut by ravines thick with dogwood and live oak. The central basin was two miles, or more, across, a narrow stream angling through the centre like the spine of a turtle when the shell is upturned and the body opened.

The Cheyenne watched the wagon go past them, then disappeared from the rim of the valley as Azul led the way down to the rich grass below.

The sun curled across the sky, moving steadily towards the edge of the mountains bulking up from the west. The wagon reached the stream and the halfbreed called a halt, letting his own horse drink before taking the mules down. He waited as the animals enjoyed the unusual luxury of fresh grass. Then harnessed them again and began to push on.

The halt was chosen deliberately: if the Cheyenne had intended to attack, they would have struck then, when the wagon was most vulnerable. But there was no further sign of the watching Indians.

At least, not until Azul crested the rim of the basin.

There was a distinct trail leading out to the north, angling up the flat side of the hollow to a place where the surrounding ridge split apart. Azul rode up the trail to the highest point, where it crested the spine of primeval rock and began to slant down to the badlands beyond.

As he halted the big stallion, scanning the way ahead, Indians appeared from both sides of the rock.

They were dressed like the nine he had seen before, but now the number was swelled up to fourteen. Six held rifles, while the others carried bows and lances. They came out from the trees flanking the pass to form a line across his path. He noticed that only six warriors blocked the trail, the others just sitting their ponies on the downswing of the ridges. He noticed, too, that the Cheyenne knew how to plan an ambush: the men facing him were the ones with the fire-power to kill him fast; the warriors on the slopes were those with lances and bows, the angles of the ground allowing them an advantage of speed and cover that was denied him.

He kept his hands away from his guns.

A warrior with an eagle feather bonnet moved his pony out in front of the others. His hair hung down beside his temples in heavy plaits that were bound with coloured cloth and beads. He wore a hide shirt with a quill breast-plate; a loin-cloth, and tight leggings that were fringed with badger's bristles and fox's fur. He rode a piebald mustang, the shoulders imprinted with the mark of a dyed hand and the mane wound through with shells and beads. He had a shield slung behind his left thigh, and a quiver of arrows at the front. A bone bow protruded from its sheath behind his right shoulder.

But the Winchester carbine he pointed casually in Azul's direction was the most dangerous weapon.

He barked a question that Azul couldn't understand. Then tried to speak English when the halfbreed shrugged and made sign to indicate he didn't know what was being said.

A second man came forwards when the one with the bonnet turned and shouted a gutteral order. He wore a headdress made from the skull of a buffalo, the hide drooping about his face and the pelt hanging down over his back. He wore only a quill breast-plate and a loin-cloth, his body otherwise bare, apart from the fox-fur moccasins, the tails still attached so that they hung down past his pony's ribs, almost touching the ground.

He carried no weapons other than a tomahawk and a knife, but his hands were filled with several rattles made from the tails of snakes and the skulls of animals, the openings into the bone blocked by clay and inset with shiny glass.

'Why do you come here?'

It was hard for Azul to understand the words, because they were pitched to the Cheyenne dialect, so that they sounded like, *Kie yook heer.*

'*Hablar Espanol?*'

The man in the buffalo headdress grunted and spat.

Azul shrugged: 'I don't speak Cheyenne, either.'

He pointed back at the wagon. 'I am taking them north. We don't want to stop. Just go through to what the white men call Wyoming.'

There was a sudden hissing from the Indians.

'You go the Black Hills,' said the interpreter. 'Too many go there.'

'No,' Azul replied. 'I never heard of the Black Hills.'

'You not hear of Pa-ha-sa-phe?'

He shook his head. 'I'm just taking these women north. To Wyoming. I never heard of those hills you talk about. We don't want to stop, just to go to a town called Jericho.'

'Jericho?' It came out as *He-rick-o.* 'You go there?'

'Yes.' Azul wondered why the Indians all laughed. 'I was hired to take the women there.'

'The two on the wagon?' said the buffalo-headed man. 'You are taking them to Jericho?'

Azul nodded. 'They have people there. The old woman's husband is dead, so they are going to join her family.'

The Cheyenne laughed again.

Azul wondered why. But he said, 'Will you let them go through? They do not intend to stop. All they want is to get to Jericho.'

Again, like an often-told joke, the name of the town raised

laughter amongst the Indians.

The man in the headdress translated the message to the others. The warrior in the eagle-feathered bonnet listened, then stared at Azul and nodded his head.

The horns that stuck out from the buffalo skin ducked up and down. The brown face beneath danced in turn, the lips parting to emit a throaty chuckle. The warriors behind shook their lances, rattling the poles against the stressed hide of their shields.

'Yes,' said the buffalo man. 'You can go on to Jericho. We shall not stop you.'

'You have my thanks,' said Azul. 'And the thanks of the women.'

'Small gratitude for broken walls,' murmured the buffalo man. 'Thank me later, when you see what you go to.'

'I do not understand your words,' said Azul. 'Are you giving me a warning?'

'I have told you that we shall not block your path,' said the man. 'Ride on to Jericho, and we will send word to our brothers not to stop you.'

He laughed, grunting a sentence at the warriors in the eagle-feathered bonnet. Then all the Cheyenne turned away, disappearing over the ridges like day-time ghosts fading into a night that was lit bright by the sun.

Azul rode back to the wagon.

'They won't stop us,' he said. 'They gave their word.'

'And you believe them?' Grace demanded. 'You trust those savages?'

'They gave their word.' Azul nodded. 'Yeah: I trust them.'

'Trust one, trust any. They're all the same.' Grace looked towards her mother. 'We should have used the railroad and the stage coach.'

'Hush up, daughter.' Hope Walls turned to Azul. 'You really think they'll let us go through?'

'I said so.' Azul's voice got hard and cold. 'They gave their word.'

He looked at Grace: 'And I trust that better than a white man's promise.'

'Well' The dark-haired woman took a deep breath, bunching her shoulders as she stared at the horizon. 'I've been insulted before, but I'm not ready to take it from a gainsaid halfbreed.'

'I wasn't offering,' said Azul. 'You get it from who you like. Just don't screw up the people with you.'

Chapter Six

They entered the badlands, their passage slowed by the nature of the terrain. The trail, although remaining relatively straight, became more difficult to negotiate as the folds of the country broke it into a series of ridges and hollows. The mules strained up the rises and plodded down the slopes, Hope Walls keeping one foot jammed tight against the brake to prevent the wagon sliding down over the animals. They moved from sunlight into shade, and then out again, only to enter another pool of darkness as they hit the next dip.

There was no more sign of the Cheyenne, but both women remained nervous. Azul did not allow it to show, but he was not certain of the Indians' intentions.

There had been a mocking aspect to their permission that the wagon be allowed to cross their territory, a group amusement at the destination. Azul wondered if they were playing some kind of macabre joke. It was difficult to tell, given the barrier created by the language gap, but the mention of Jericho had definitely raised laughter amongst them: as though the name itself was some kind of private joke. And the halfbreed knew – if the Cheyenne were anything at all like the Apache – how gruesome that joke might be.

Once, after a bunch of Mexicans had crossed the border to raid a string of *rancherias*, taking away around a dozen women and killing about nine men, Azul had ridden with a warrior band in pursuit of vengeance. The Mexicans had been well-armed, and mounted on good horses. In addition, they held the women and several children as hostages. The band of pursuers was made up of Chiricahua and Mimbreño warriors, led by a young war chief called Lynx. They had picked up the Mexicans' trail easily enough, but not been able to outdistance the raiders: the Mexicans had taken refuge in a tiny village, close under the northern reach of the Sierra Madre.

Lynx had then ordered his warriors to round up every *peon* they could find within a night's ride of the *pueblo*. The tally came to seven men and eleven women. The Apaches had spent the night cutting poles so that as the sun rose over the *pueblo*, the inhabitants could see the luckless farmers lashed upright to X-shaped crosses. Each one was naked, with a bonfire built up as high as their ankles, a man standing beside the dry wood with a lit torch in his hand.

Then Lynx had ridden up to the edge of the village with a piece of white cloth tied to his bow, and demanded the release of the Apache prisoners. He had promised that the *pueblo* should remain unharmed if the women and children were released.

'What will you do to the others?' the *jefe* had asked. 'How can we trust you?'

'Let the ones who took our women come out,' Lynx had replied. 'Let them bring our people out and set them free. Then they can take your people back. We shall not attack them while they do this.'

The raiders had not enjoyed the idea, but the people of the village forced them out, bringing the Apache women and children with them. The Apaches had stood watching as all their people were freed, then waited until the Mexicans were gone back inside the village.

Lynx had gone up to the houses again – Azul had thought he was overly confident, and too boastful, but no one fired at him – and said, 'Thank you. You have given us back what belongs to us. But not all.'

'What else do you want?' the *jefe* had shouted. 'What else can we give you?'

'Give back the lives of the men they killed,' Lynx had

answered. 'Bring them back to life and we shall ride away.'

'Dead men cannot be returned to life,' was the reply. 'We have sent you your women, now leave us alone.'

'Life demands life,' Lynx had said. And turned his pony, ignoring the bullets that danced dust around the mustang's feet.

While all this was going on, five warriors had crept into the village and lit a fire in the mission there. By the time it took firm hold of the beams and began to crack the sun-dried adobe of the roof and walls, so that the plaster baked black and began to crack and fall down, the Apache women were safely away, escorted by five warriors.

The villagers had put out the blaze and demanded that the men responsible for the outrage chase the *indios*. After all, they were the ones who had brought the dreaded Apaches down on the *pueblo*.

The raiders had come out. There were twelve of them, each one armed with a pistol and a rifle.

They had come out fast, riding fresh horses at full gallop.

Lynx had stationed men all around the village so that all the warriors might join together to hunt the Mexicans down.

They had waited until the entire band was gathered, then gone after the raiders. They waited for half a day, then rode slowly behind the Mexicans. They had caught up with them around midnight and killed them all, taking their guns and ammunition and hair.

The next day Lynx had ordered each warrior to take a scalp and ride in close to the village, tossing the bloody hair over the walls and into the streets as he went by.

It was a great joke, for none had fired a shot at the *pueblo*. Or an arrow. Or thrown a tomahawk, or a knife. But the villagers had learned what it meant to cross the Apache tribes.

And afterwards the story was told, and retold, around the fires, when the nights got long and the air cold. And Lynx had been hailed as a man with honour, a brave warrior, with a sense of humour.

And now Azul remembered. And wondered if the Cheyenne were planning some similar joke.

But afternoon became twilight and then night. And dawn followed, without attack, so that he decided he was right in his first estimation: that the word of the Plains Indians was good, and the wagon was truly granted free passage to Jericho.

They reached Pueblo. Which was a huddled cluster of timber and clay buildings, many of them falling down now that the railroad had taken the cream off the top of the cattle trade.

The bright iron lines had been built to Trinidad and Santa Fe, curling on down to Albuquerque and El Paso, so that there was no longer any need to drive Texas steers up to the headwaters of the Arkansas, where before the riverboats had shipped the cattle eastwards. The stock yards were empty, the cattle all gone. And only the memory of glory lingered on, along with the stink the herds had left behind.

The town was dead: a withered thing that clutched the prairie in its last gasps, refusing to recognise the fact of its dying.

They stopped overnight, the two women sleeping in a moderately clean hotel while Azul slept inside the wagon. It was the first real chance he had had to study the interior at leisure. When they had halted in Taos, their rooms had overlooked the corral behind and the halfbreed had eased the conestoga up close against the windows. In Trinidad, they had halted just long enough to replenish their supplies, wary of stopping over for fear of another attack. And on the trail, the women occupied the wagon, Azul sleeping in the open.

But now the mules needed rest, so the halfbreed got his chance.

Hope Walls pointed out the box she said contained the

documents. It was a small wooden container, the sides and lid banded with metal strips, fastened by a sturdy padlock. It was hidden inside a larger trunk, covered with clothes, but not so well hidden that a diligent searcher would miss it – if he knew what he was looking for. Azul still doubted that it was the real reason for the attacks, but could see nothing else that might prompt anyone to hire gunmen to halt their passage.

After dinner he squatted down inside the conestoga, thinking about the problem.

The story Hope had told him was plausible enough, but somehow – for no reason he could clearly define – he doubted it. If someone – possibly a relative of Hope's – had learnt of her intention to travel north to join her brother, then they must also have known where she was coming from, let alone her exact destination. That had to mean it was easier to halt the wagon either at the start of its journey or at the end. To hire men to wait along the trail was both costly and time-consuming, with no sure guarantee of success. So: someone was prepared to spend a good deal of money – three thousand dollars, Bennett had said – on preventing the women from reaching Jericho, or on obtaining the box.

The more he thought about it, the less likely it seemed.

He decided to search the conestoga.

It was a typical prairie schooner: the bed around fourteen feet long and maybe five wide, with the raised walls flanked by a series of hickory bows that supported the canvas. The wheels were bonded with iron tyres, and the only unusual feature was the thickness of the wood itself. The interior was jammed tight and high with stacked furniture, roped in position against the jolting of the trail. There was a spinola and a set of fancy chairs; a circular table of some exotic wood and a pine dresser; trunks contained clothing and the small appurtenances of domestic life: cutlery and crockery, linen, glasses. Azul gave each chest a brief examination and found nothing. He checked the underside, noticing that the bed of the wagon – like the sides – was unusually thick, the wood painted with creosote as protection against the elements. That, he thought, might account for the unusual weight of the vehicle.

But it did not satisfy his curiosity.

Nor did anything else and he was forced to settle down for the night with his suspicions still unanswered.

He slept inside, for a cutting wind had gotten up in the north and was blowing hard down the edge of the Rockies, battering at the canvas so that the material trembled and cracked like the sails of a ship. The central part of the floor was cleared of furniture and spread with a treble layer of thick blankets. Cushions were piled at the forward end, and there were more blankets in an open box behind the seat. Azul laced the openings at front and back shut and settled down to sleep.

With the practical stoicism of his mother's people, he pushed the doubts from his mind and concentrated on resting his body. Whatever the answers might be, they would become apparent in time, so for now there was no point in wasting time on idle speculation.

He slept soundly, undisturbed by the wind or any prowlers.

Morning dawned cold and still. The wind had ceased, but the temperature had dropped considerably, leaving the ground hard and frosted with a covering of ice that sparkled in the early sun.

Azul rose, shivering, and sluiced water from the pump behind the saloon over his torso and face. He pulled on a heavy jacket of dark blue cloth, hip-length, and then went inside the saloon.

After a while, Hope and Grace appeared, wrapped up in woollens. They ate breakfast and then continued on their journey.

According to the maps they had purchased the trail went on to Colorado Springs and then to Denver. After that, it followed the line of the Kansas Pacific railroad to Cheyenne, which stood just over the border between the territories of Colorado and Wyoming. Beyond the town, the country was empty, the contour lines indicating a landscape of rolling plains interspersed with mountains. Hope Walls indicated a spot just south of the Montana border, between two rivers called the Tongue and Powder. To the east was a range of hills called the Bighorn Mountains.

'There,' she said, proudly, 'that's where Joshua built his town. How long do you think it will take?'

Azul shrugged. 'A month. Maybe longer. It depends on the trail.'

He pointed at a river, tracing its course until he found the name: The North Platte. 'That might be a problem, or the Powder.' He tapped the black line indicating the second river's course across central Wyoming. 'But let's worry about that when we get there. It doesn't look too difficult.'

'What about the Indians?'

'Depends on how much influence the ones we met have,' said Azul. 'I don't know which tribes ride north of here. Or how they feel about travellers.'

Grace frowned and muttered something about guides who didn't know the country. Azul ignored her, by now accustomed to her jibes. 'Sooner we get moving,' he said, 'the sooner we'll find out.'

They quit Pueblo and pushed on northwards.

Beyond the town the Rockies pushed a spur out that forced them to detour in a wide swing around the jumbled stone. The women were all for taking a direct line, chancing a broken axle crossing the raw granite, but Azul persuaded them otherwise, pointing out that the flatter path would more than compensate for the difficulties of traversing the rocks. The detour swung them wide of Colorado Springs so that they missed the town completely, angling north and west in the direction of Denver.

The going was easy after the slow ride up from New Mexico. The ground stayed firm, still partially frozen, but with the first warmth of spring leavening the chill so that grass sprouted afresh in the sunnier areas, and the trees began to form green buds. It was a mightily different terrain to the landscapes Azul knew. The southwest was a land of high mountains and hidden meadows, the plateaux mostly dry in summer and snow-clad in winter: a land of extremes. Here, the plains stretched away in seemingly endless undulations, like a shaken blanket frozen in mid-movement. The Rockies shadowed them to the west, the enormous bulk of the Great Divide never more impressive than when seen from the flatlands below, while ahead and to the east there was nothing but the rolling plain.

Occasionally they saw smoke, and sometimes groups of Indians watched them from the distance. But there was no attack and after ten days they came into Denver.

Azul was cautious of the town, for it seemed an obvious place to ambush the wagon. The lines of the Kansas Pacific ran westwards across Colorado to join the line of the South Platte river there, following the water northwards before continuing over the plains to Cheyenne. Travellers moving up from the south would almost certainly pass through, and Denver was not so large that a conestoga manned by two women and a halfbreed might go unnoticed. But they needed fresh supplies and the mules could use a rest: the necessities outweighed the dangers.

Denver spread in a huddle of buildings along the line of the river. Where the town flanked the banks of the South Platte, the buildings were mostly warehouses and stockyards. A sprawl of cabins banded the place on the south, giving way to the tracks of the railroad and the main area of the depot. Beyond, confined by the river and the rails, was the centre of town. Over it, there hung a stench of death.

It was like riding into a massive charnel house, the air thick with the smell of blood and decaying flesh. The women gagged, clutching handkerchiefs to their faces in a vain attempt to fend off the penetrating odour.

'My God!' Grace screwed up her pretty face as she addressed Azul. 'What is it?'

The halfbreed pointed to the west, where great piles of bones were stacked. The day was warm, and rain had fallen recently so that the snow was melting from the bleak monuments.

'Buffalo hunters.' He spat, trying to empty his mouth of the sour taste that seemed to fill it. 'They kill all through the summer an' leave the carcasses out on the prairie for the skinners to bring in. Now the railroad's come through, I guess they're shipping the bones to the east.'

'It's awful.' Grace pressed the kerchief back against her mouth and nose, so Azul couldn't tell if she referred to the wanton slaughter or the smell. He guessed the latter.

They reached the centre of town, where a wide street ran from south to north, bisected at intervals by smaller avenues and narrow alleyways. The stench was less noticeable here, though it was impossible to escape it completely for it hung in the air, permeating the timbers of the buildings and the clothes of the citizens. Most of all, it tainted the clothes and hair and skin of the hunters themselves. They were hard-looking men, with long hair and a mixture of clothing that ranged from newly-bought suits to fringed buckskins. Many still carried the big Sharps carbines – the ·50 calibre buffalo guns – they used to kill the shaggy bison, though the skinners and teamsters tended to retain the basic tools of their bloody trade: long-bladed knives and plaited bull-hide whips. All wore side-arms. Colts were the most prominent, either the long-barrelled Cavalry model or the shorter Frontier model that Azul himself carried; but there were also Remingtons and Smith & Wesson revolvers, even a sprinkling of much older pistols. Cap and ball guns converted to cartridge loading, or retained in their original form so that the men walked with pouches of lead balls and flasks of powder strung from their belts.

They filled up the sidewalks, jostling the regular citizens or sleeping off their drunks in the chairs that fronted the saloons and stores.

The citizens either ignored them or attempted to lure them

inside whatever emporium they happened to pause beside – from cathouses to gunsmiths – with little success. The buffalo hunters were waiting out the winter. Waiting until the herds moved north again and the new season's killing might begin. Until then, they would hold on to whatever they had not already spent in favour of liquor and women, the latter coming second to the first.

Azul spotted a deputy sheriff lounging against a storefront and reined in alongside.

The deputy was short, but built wide, with a broken nose and small black eyes that never stopped in one place for very long. He wore a cloth coat with a gunbelt fastened around the waist, the butt of a Colt protruding from the holster. He carried a Winchester shotgun in his folded arms. And looked at the halfbreed like he was ready to take an argument.

Azul noticed that he kept a finger on the right-hand trigger and his thumb on the hammer.

'Need a decent hotel,' he said. 'Where two ladies can stay.'

The deputy chuckled and arched a gobbet of tobacco-stained spittle into the street.

'What kinda ladies? Night-time women, or decent folk?'

'Decent.' Azul glanced back, motioning for Hope to halt the wagon. 'Respectable folk.'

The deputy chuckled again: 'That makes a change. Ain't been nothing come through lately that anyone could call respectable. Less you make the difference between them 'as got the pox an' them without.'

'Clean,' grunted Azul, holding on to his temper. 'Honest women going north.'

'Yeah.' The deputy eased his left hand far enough away from the shotgun to drag a plug of tobacco from his coat and bite off a hunk. He chewed for a bit, then said: 'To where?'

'Not your business,' rasped Azul. 'I just want a place to stay. Someplace clean.'

The shotgun canted over to point on Azul's chest. And the deputy said, 'Don't give me no lip, feller. I ask a question, you give the answer. 'Less you want a charge o' buckshot messin' up that pretty coat you wear.'

Azul dropped the reins of the big grey and lifted his hands.

'No trouble, mister. I'm just the guide.'

The deputy stared at him. 'You're a 'breed, ain't you? Never could stand squawmen's brats.'

Azul climbed down from the stallion, dismounting Indian style: on the right.

'I knew I got it,' said the deputy. 'You can always tell a squaw-bastard by the way he rides.'

'You can always tell a bastard,' Azul murmured, coming round the front of the ground-hitched horse. 'By the way he talks.'

'What?' The deputy sounded surprised. 'What's that mean?'

'Means you're a bastard,' rasped Azul. 'With a lesson to learn.'

The deputy began to lower his shotgun, but then Hope Walls shouted, 'For godsakes, don't make trouble!'

The deputy turned, staring at the wagon. He saw a grey-haired old lady, her face nut-brown from the sun, creased with wrinkles. Dressed in black. Hands tensed on the traces so that the veins stood out on the backs like the tracks of time carved on the memory of youth.

Then he saw Grace: her hair pulled back under a red ribbon that accentuated the pure raven-darkness; the green eyes and the sensual mouth. She had dropped her shawl so that her blouse was exposed. It was open almost to her waist, in answer to the early heat. Her breasts swelled against the material, providing a focus of attention that occupied all of the deputy's mind as Azul climbed the steps on to the boardwalk.

'When you done looking,' said the halfbreed, 'I've got something for you.'

Hope dropped the traces and said, 'No!'

Grace smiled. Saying nothing.

The deputy sheriff tore his eyes away from Grace's cleavage as Azul's right hand came forwards to grasp the twin-barrels of the shotgun and point the weapon away. At the same time, the halfbreed's left foot clamped down over the deputy's boot, and his right knee lifted into the man's groin.

The deputy screamed, doubling over with both hands clutching at the source of his pain. The shotgun went off spreading a charge against the underside of the porch as Azul dragged the gun clear from the short man's grip.

Shards of plaster and wood fell down like solid rain. People in the street halted now, turning to watch. Azul broke the gun open and thumbed the unspent cartridge clear. Tossed it across the street, then hurled the scattergun in the opposite direction.

The deputy began reaching for the pistol on his hip. Azul kicked him in the same place. Then again in the groin. The pistol spun clear of the deputy's hand. Azul kicked him in the face.

He felt teeth break, and moved clear as blood spurted from the peace-officer's mouth.

A buffalo hunter shouted applause and Azul realised that he was surrounded by an audience of grinning men.

'He goddamn deserved that,' someone said. 'Bastard's been riding too hard.'

'Yeah. Jumped up little cock.'

'Ain't crowing too loud now, though.'

'Sounds more like one o' them gelded cocks. Makes noise, but can't do much.'

'Hey! That just leaves him good fer throwin' eggs.' Someone pointed at the dark smear that stained the deputy's pants. 'An' he's doin' that right now.'

There was a hoot of laughter. Azul ignored it, climbing back on the grey and leading the way up the street.

'He'll come looking for you,' called Hope. 'Soon as he recovers.'

'I know it,' said Azul. 'But next time he'll be more careful. He'll know what to expect.'

'Was it on account of us?' asked the grey-haired lady. 'Or because he insulted your kin?'

'Bit of both, ma'am,' Azul replied. 'He insulted us both. An' I was raised by a Christian father.'

'And an Indian mother,' added Grace. 'He was right, in one way.'

'He called me a bastard,' said Azul. 'But my parents were married. I didn't like the insult.'

'Was that reason to cripple him?' Grace demanded. 'The way you kicked him, he'll never have children.'

'So he'll never have the problem, either,' grunted Azul.

'What problem?' Grace demanded. 'I don't understand.'

'No.' Azul's face was set hard as they rode along the street, ignoring the crowd that gathered about the crippled deputy. 'But he won't be in doubt anymore.'

Chapter Seven

They found rooms in the most expensive hotel around. It had its own stable built out back of the three-storey building with a permanent watchman on duty at the gates and a man always inside the main barn. Azul saw the grey stallion safely into a pen and then checked the wagon. He slipped the watchman ten of Hope Walls's dollars to take special care of the wagon and his own promise of retribution should anything happen to the vehicle, then went to eat.

The conversation during the meal accentuated his suspicions, adding to his doubts about the women.

'Your behaviour today got us noticed,' said Grace.

Her eyes were angry over the soup spoon she lifted delicately to her lips.

'I have to go along,' said Hope. 'You could've taken care of the bastard later.'

'Mother!' Grace spilled the warm liquid from her spoon on to the table. 'Please!'

'I've heard you talk worse,' said Hope. 'Back in Galenas?'

'Mother! Please!'

Grace held her voice down to a ladylike level, dabbing at her lips with a napkin. But the flash of her green eyes and the angry note in her voice showed that her mother had hit a sore point.

Azul said nothing. Instead he wondered what difference existed between them. Hope wore widow's weeds and altered her speech to the occasion, slipping from the exactitude of a well-brought-up woman to the slipshod parlance of the Frontier. Grace favoured fancy dresses and fancy talk. She knew nothing about horses or guns. And appeared to take exception to any kind of rough talk, or travelling.

Azul wondered what she had done in Galenas.

Hope Walls overcame the difficult moment by suggesting that they all retire to bed. Azul agreed, following the women up the stairs to their room on the first floor. His own was on the second level: a small square of scrubbed pinewood with a narrow bed and a washstand; a trio of hooks nailed against the far wall and a window overlooking the corral behind the hotel.

He stripped off, looping his gunbelt over the bedhead and canting the Winchester against the wall alongside. He tucked the throwing knife under the pillow, and settled down to sleep.

He was awakened by the boot that smashed against the flimsy lock and swung the door inwards. The sound of the heel thudding against the lock lifted him up from unconsciousness in time to grasp the throwing knife as the door splintered out from the frame.

He lifted upright as a bulky figure came in through the door and flung the knife overhand. It struck as he twisted, reaching for the Colt, entering the shape that was blocking out the light between the lower curve of the ribs and the gleaming buckle on the man's belt.

The man screamed and dropped something heavy on to the floor as he staggered back with both hands plucking at the hilt of the blade protruding from his belly. He cannoned into the men behind him, and sat down, his moans pitched up high as he fought to drag the knife clear of his gut.

Azul yanked the Colt clear of the holster and triggered three shots into the dim-lit corridor.

A man screamed, clutching at his face. And another simply grunted as he was blasted back against the far wall. He hit a door that burst inwards under his weight and crashed down over the threadbare carpet with blood pumping from the holes in his chest. A woman shrieked as the door opened, then a man shouted and began firing a pistol into the corridor.

Azul ducked under the bed as the bullets whistled through his room. He heard the window behind him shatter, and felt the coolness of the glass on his bare legs. He emptied his pistol at the feet around the doorway.

Saw a heel blown clear of one man's boot so that he fell down and caught a bullet in the buttocks, and saw another man's ankle blown apart. He dropped the Colt and grabbed for the Winchester.

The man with the smashed ankle was yelling and clutching at his leg. Until a shot from across the corridor hit him in the face, spraying a sticky mess of bone and blood over Azul's bed. Then he stopped wimpering and slumped back, gazing sightlessly at the ceiling as blood ran down his face from the hole where his nose had been.

The other one rolled on to his belly, angling a Smith & Wesson Schofield across the room. Azul triggered the Winchester. Levered and triggered again.

The first shot exploded the Smith & Wesson, striking the cylinder so that the whole chamber detonated back into the man's face. Abruptly it was stripped of flesh, only the blind eyes and the wide-open, screaming mouth left to remind the gathering onlookers that once the screeching thing had been human. The second shot hit his throat. It blasted in through his adam's apple and then ricocheted off his spine to emerge from under his left ear. The stripped and bleeding face jerked back, spouting blood in thick sprays from the multiple wounds. Then it slammed forwards, dropping to the floor as the voice cut off. Little spurts of blood still pulsed from the neck.

There was the sound of running feet. A shout, closely followed by a shot. Then a scream and the sound of a door slamming closed.

Azul stood up, pointing the Winchester at the door. A woman gasped, 'My God! He's naked!' Another murmured, 'Yeah.' He dragged a sheet from the bed and draped it around his waist. It was splattered with the blood of the ankle-shot killer.

From across the way a tall man pushed through the crowd. He wore only a pair of faded jeans, but when the onlookers saw him they backed away. He stopped at Azul's door and glanced down at the five corpses.

'You don't seem too popular, feller.'

'No.' Azul shrugged. 'Don't know why. But thanks for helping out.'

'My job.' The big man grinned, running a hand through his dark hair as he stared at the man with the knife in his belly. 'I'm the marshal. John T. McLain. Besides, I don't take kindly to havin' my pleasure disturbed.'

Azul lowered the rifle. 'All right if I get dressed?'

McLain nodded. 'Sure. Go ahead. Guess I'd better, too. I'll hafta speak with you. Down at my office.'

He glanced at the dying man again, and said: 'See you there in thirty minutes. Maybe you'll have some answers by then.'

Azul nodded. 'Maybe.'

'Fine.' McLain eased the assassin's legs clear of the door and swung it shut. Azul could hear him yelling at the crowd to disperse as he dragged the man over to the centre of the room.

The man was fat from months of excess drinking, but he still gave off the typical stench of a buffalo hunter. He was in his thirties, his fat face hidden behind a long growth of beard and shoulder length hair, both greasy. He wore a pair of broadcloth pants and an ill-matched jacket of the same material, held up by the now-empty gunbelt. His shirt was yellow, but around the midriff it was darkened by the outpouring of his blood. He moaned as the halfbreed hauled him across the bare floor, leaving behind a trail of mingled blood and urine.

'What you gonna do?'

His pale grey eyes were wide open with terror, and spittle flecked his lips.

'Take the knife out,' said Azul. 'If you answer some questions.'

'Suppose I don't?' The man's eyes got cunning through the pain and the fear. 'You can't kill me now.'

Azul shrugged. 'I can go talk with the marshal. Leave you here.'

'I'll die! Oh Sweet Jesus Christ! I'll die!'

'Yeah,' said Azul. 'That's right.'

The fat man swallowed hard. Then coughed, pressing both hands to his belly. No blood came from his mouth and Azul realised that the layers of fat had cushioned the worst of the knife's pain: the injury was not really serious, being more of a flesh wound than anything likely to kill.

But he left the blade where it was.

'Start with your name,' he said, shrugging into his clothes. 'I only got thirty minutes.'

'Nathan Durant. My friends call me Nat.'

Azul buttoned his shirt. 'I'm not a friend, Nathan. Who hired you?'

'Art Jones.' Durant squirmed, staring at his blood-stained hands. 'But he's dead now. You put a goddam bullet in his face.'

Azul belted his pants tight and shucked them inside his moccasins. 'Why?'

Durant groaned. 'I don't know why.'

Azul swung his vest over his shoulders. 'How come? Don't you ask questions when you're hired to kill a man?'

'I'm flat broke.' Sweat poured down the pudgy cheeks. 'I lost all my money on a deck o' cards.'

Azul belted his gun around his waist: 'I don't believe you.'

'Jesus Christ! It's true!' Durant went on sweating and moaning. 'I swear to God it's true!'

'That's tough.' Azul fastened the thigh-strap of the holster down. 'Looks like I have to leave that blade in your gut.'

'No! Please. Don't do that.'

Durant sweated some more as the halfbreed laced his moccasins tight and picked up his hat.

'Levi Brown! He set us up to do it. Bastard never could

plan a thing right. He never told us McLain would be across the way.'

'Who's Levi Brown?' asked Azul, gently.

'The deputy you bust up.' Durant's chubby face got ugly with pain, and sweat began to run over his jowels to mingle with the drying blood on his wide belly. 'He gave us all twenty dollars to kill you.'

Azul squatted down in front of the man and tapped the hilt of the throwing knife. 'There's five men dead, not counting you. That makes,' he counted on his fingers, 'one hundred dollars.'

Durant moaned some more as the halfbreed batted the knife.

'Why?' Azul asked again. 'He could've rigged a charge against me if he's a deputy. Why hire you? Especially at one hundred and twenty dollars. That's better than two months pay.'

'I don't know.' Durant moaned. 'That's what we got offered. Please take the knife out.'

'Who was the last man?' demanded Azul. 'The one who got away?'

'Billy Judge,' gasped the fat man. 'At least I think it was him.'

'What's he look like?'

'Short. Fair hair. Carries a fancy belt with a Remington's Army.' The flabby body heaved, fighting against the pain. 'Now will you take this sticker outta me?'

'In a while,' said Azul. 'Tell me first where Levi Brown lives.'

'Oh, God! He stays in the Resthouse. Him an' Billy, both. They shack together. You know?'

'No,' said Azul.

'They're like that,' said Durant. 'Dirty funny, if you know what I mean.'

He lifted one hand clear of the knife to shake it limp-wristed about his spreading gut.

'Like that.'

'Where's the Resthouse?' Azul demanded.

'Two blocks from the goddamned marshal's office,' replied Durant. 'You turn left an' spot it from the funny lights.'

'Thanks,' said Azul. 'Thanks a lot.'

'That mean you'll call me a doctor?'

'No.'

Azul reached out to grasp the hilt of the throwing knife. Got hold of the leather-wrapped hilt. And twisted it. Went on twisting it in a tight circle that cut round and up between the confines of Durant's ribs and pelvic girdle. The knife came free in a massive spill of blood and entrails. Durant opened his mouth in readiness of a scream, but the shock of seeing his belly spilling out before him froze his cry, so that he just sat there, trying to shove his gusting intestines back inside his stomach.

Azul wiped the blade on the sheets and stepped clear of the slumping body.

He sheathed the knife back in his moccasin and picked up his gear.

Hope and Grace Wells were waiting for him on the next level.

'I need to talk with the marshal,' he said. 'Why don't you go get the wagon ready? In case we got more trouble.'

'Is that your answer to everything?' Grace looked good in a nightdress. 'Kill and run?'

'I'm just thinking of you,' said Azul. 'You want that wagon stopped there? Or do you want to move on?'

Grace blushed, and Hope Walls pulled her back inside their room. As he went downstairs Azul could hear them arguing . . .

'He's just a killer . . .'

'But he's our guide . . .'

'Why not someone else?'

'He's the best we got. He's good.'

He went out through the doors into the moonlit street.

Frost covered the sidewalks and the roads, laying a

crackling carpet of dancing white over wood and earth alike. A cold wind blew down from the north, bristling the uppermost crystals of the frost to sparkling luminescence against the glow of the few lights still shining.

One of them was the lantern hung out above the marshal's office.

It swung in the wind, shafting cautious flashes over the dark shine of the windows. Like a smuggler's lamp luring an unwary ship on to the rocks.

Azul loaded his Colt and his Winchester as he walked down the street.

Then knocked on the door.

John T. McLain was inside, settled back behind his desk with a single barrel Meteor shotgun pointing at the door and a smile on his face.

'I didn't think you'd run,' he said. 'I counted on that.'

'Durant is dead,' said Azul. 'By now. He said he was hired by one of your deputies. Billy Judge got away.'

'Who was the deputy?' asked McLain. 'Give me his name, an' I'll bust him. Every which way but loose.'

'Levi Brown,' Durant named him and this guy called Billy Judge.' Azul began to trust the lawman. 'He said it before he died.'

'All right.' McLain stood up from behind his desk. 'Let's go talk with Levi Brown.'

'And Billy Judge,' said Azul. 'They sleep together. In the Resthouse. Seems like they like it like that.'

'So we'll split their partnership up,' grunted McLain. 'I never figured my deputy for queer.'

'I don't know,' said Azul, 'perhaps he isn't.'

'We'll check, anyway,' said McLain. 'Just to be sure.'

'Your choice,' Azul replied. 'It's always best to test the fruit.'

'What fruit?' McLain asked.

'The rotten ones,' Azul said. 'The ones that spoil the barrel.'

'Trouble is spotting them,' grunted McLain. 'How'd you do that?'

'Just watch them,' said Azul drily. 'They come out brown.'

Chapter Eight

The Resthouse was a two-storey frame building with a neat porch over which some kind of climbing plant was growing. The foliage was thick enough that it almost obscured the purple-masked lanterns hung behind, diffusing the light into a myriad patterns that flickered through the shrouding creeper and shed a strange radiance over the frosty ground.

McLain went in through the main door with Azul close behind. The big marshal had the Meteor holstered on his left hip now, the cut-down barrel sitting snug inside a specially-designed leather loop. Azul noticed that the stock was cut away, so that only the pistol grip remained. McLain wore a Colt's Frontier on his right hip, his hand never far from the butt. Azul held the Winchester, a cartridge in the chamber and his thumb on the hammer.

The interior of the rooming house gave off a cloying scent that seemed made up of a mingling of sweat, tobacco smoke and perfume. The walls of the vestibule were papered in some kind of plush material, gold *fleur de lys* picked out against the scarlet. There were two chairs covered in the same material, and a small desk.

McLain punched the bell.

'Smells like a New Orleans cathouse,' grunted the marshal. 'But I don't see no girls.'

'You wouldn't.' The voice was soft, lisping. 'Nasty creatures.'

'Depends on your tastes,' snapped McLain. 'We ain't all cornholers.'

'Boys will be boys, dear.'

The man was around thirty, with thinning hair grown long

and twisted into curls. His eyes were very bright, the paleness of the pupils accentuated by the carefully-applied mascara. His mouth was puckered up in a pout. The lips looked as though they were rouged. He wore a yellow dressing-gown with small, red flowers embroidered on it: a reversal of the main colour scheme.

'Listen, you goddamn faggot!' McLain stepped towards the man.

'Marshal! Please!' A languid hand flapped a scented handkerchief in the air. 'It's a free country, isn't it? Why, I've heard of people who do things with animals. With pigs and sheep! Cows, even!'

'Get shafted,' snarled McLain.

'Promises, promises.' The man simpered. 'Do you and your friend want a room?'

'Yeah.' McLain reached out to grab the front of the ornate gown, twisting the cloth so that the man's head was forced back and his feet were dragged partway off the floor. 'Levi Brown's room.'

'The deputy.' The man fought hard to retain his composure. 'He stays with Billy Judge.'

McLain twisted harder.

'In room seven. This floor. Down the corridor.'

'Thanks.' McLain released his grip. 'Thanks a lot.'

'Any time. Especially if you change your mind. Or your lovely friend.'

Azul grinned, the smile producing a flutter of the darkened eye lashes. Then he moved forwards. Fast. Lifting the Winchester in a double-handed grip that slammed the stock into the queer's side. The man squealed and fell back against the desk, doubling over. Azul swung the rifle back, landing the flat of the stock along the man's temple. The shadowed eyes shut tight and the reddened mouth gaped open. The importuning clerk folded like an empty sack, collapsing in a flutter of silk that exposed the stockings covering his legs.

'Boys will be boys,' mimicked the halfbreed. 'But some play rough.'

McLain glanced at the crumpled form and pointed down the corridor. 'There's most likely a window at the back. You want to cover it?'

Azul nodded and slid through the door.

The Resthouse was flanked by alleyways on both sides, the rear enclosed by a low fence. Dustbins stood behind the building, their contents the subject of interest of numerous snarling cats. Azul kicked a big ginger tom out of his way and climbed on to the narrow porch. Like the front, it was thick with creeper, shading the windows and hiding his movements in a veil of shadow. He counted off the rooms until he reached the seventh.

When he listened at the shuttered frame he heard two men engaged in a low-voiced conversation.

'Fer Chissakes, Levi! What else could I do?'

'Kill the bastard.' The second voice was husky with pain. Azul recognised it as belonging to the deputy. 'That's what I paid you for.'

'He was too quick. He's a killer.' The second voice was whining, nasal. 'He shot Art an' put a blade in Nat. Then your boss joined in.'

'McLain?' The husky voice got stronger as a mixture of anger and fear entered the throaty tones. 'Did he see you?'

'No, Levi! I swear he didn't.' The whining voice got softer, supplicatory. 'Don't get mad. I'll make it up to you. I promise. The way you like.'

The door fronting the corridor burst open as McLain smashed his boot against the lock. Azul heard the wood splinter and jammed the rifle's barrel between the shutters. The catch snapped, its breaking hidden under the shriek of Billy Judge and the flood of curses from Levi Brown. He thrust the Winchester in through the glass, ignoring the shards that fell about his face.

'You're fired, Levi,' said McLain. 'All washed up.'

A kerosene lantern glowed at the centre of the room, suspended from the ceiling on a length of chain. The soft yellow light illuminated a double bed, the sheets bulked out by Brown's naked body. Billy Judge was backed up against a wardrobe, his hands at waist height, close to the butt of the Remington's Army model sitting in the fancy holster.

He drew the pistol as McLain entered the room.

The big lawman caught the movement and swung round, angling his own gun on the fair-haired man. The hammer of the Colt was already back, so that it needed only the pressure of the marshal's forefinger on the trigger to discharge the ·45 calibre load.

Whether McLain was trying to take the assassin alive, or if his aim was slightly off was impossible to tell. His shot struck Billy Judge on the inside of his right arm and ricocheted off the bone into the short man's side. Judge screamed and dropped his gun as blood stained the sleeve of his coat. He clapped his left hand to his side, falling down on his knees with his ugly little eyes screwed up tight.

Levi Brown rolled clear of the bed, reaching under the pillow as McLain's attention was held by the wounded man. His lips were swollen, purplish in the faint light, with the threads of stitches jutting from the lacerations inflicted by Azul's kicking. His waist was swathed in bandages. His right hand held a Colt's Peacemaker.

Azul fired without thinking: a reaction born of pure instinct.

The bullet hit Levi Brown between the shoulderblades. It smashed through the thin flesh covering the scapula and tore out high on the left side of the chest, opening a gaping hole in Brown's lung. The force of it slammed the deputy against the bed, turning his aim so that his bullet struck the wall a foot to the side of McLain. A choking scream burst from his lips, followed fast by a thick spurt of blood. He pushed himself back, trying to turn so as to bring his Colt round to level on the window.

McLain fired again.

The shot struck Brown on the left cheekbone, glancing upwards into the socket of his eye. The orb pulped under the impact, the hole filling with blood and runny matter as the slug went on into the brain.

Levi Brown jerked on his knees, rictus action triggering one last shot. Billy Judge screamed again. The bent deputy dropped his arms, slumping forwards to rest his head on the grubby sheets. The white was abruptly covered with a steady flow of red. More blood pumped, for a while, from his back, running down his pallid skin to stain the bandages and trickle sluggishly over his thighs and buttocks. A gust of wind burst from him, adding its own stink to the cordite filling the room.

Azul smashed the remainder of the window and clambered through as McLain went over to Billy Judge.

The fair-haired man was leant back against the wardrobe. Blood ran from his nostrils and mouth, dripping off his chin to join the two dark circles spread over his shirt. McLain's bullet had gone in on the right side; Levi Brown's last shot had pierced the stomach and deflected off a rib into the heart.

Billy Judge was dead.

'Goddammit!' McLain snarled. 'I wanted to ask them some questions.'

Azul shrugged. 'Let's take a look around.'

'Yeah.' The marshal slammed the door on the gaping crowd. All men. 'Let's do that.'

They took the room apart, but all they found was a letter and one thousand dollars. The letter read:

One thousand on account. The same amount if you stop them and bring the wagon to me. Keep them alive if you can.

Like the other message Azul had seen, it was unsigned.

There was no envelope to give a clue as to the origin, nor any other indication of Levi Brown's mysterious employer.

'Hell!' McLain ejected the spent shells from his Colt and thumbed fresh loads into place. 'I was hopin' we'd find something. I guess it leaves us both in the dark.'

'Yeah,' nodded the halfbreed, 'it looks that way.'

'So what you gonna do now?'

'Leave, I reckon.' Azul pushed bullets into the Winchester. 'I'm just hired to get those women through to Wyoming. Maybe there's an answer there. But I figure it's best to leave right now. We might've got Brown's friends gingered up, an' I promised to take care of the Walls women.'

'You got yourself a problem,' grunted McLain. 'If this deal's anything to go by.'

'Reckon you got your share,' grinned Azul. 'Listen.'

McLain turned as the halfbreed pointed at the door.

There was a growing surge of sound from outside. The voices sounded angry, and every so often a hand or foot rapped on the wood. McLain smiled back and set a hand on the knob.

'I might need some backing out there.'

'I'll ride herd,' said Azul. 'But don't expect me to cover you.'

'Just keep your weapon cocked,' said McLain. 'An' don't come too close behind.'

He opened the door.

The corridor was filled with men in various stages of undress. Most looked relatively normal, but several wore the same kind of female make-up the desk clerk had sported. A few carried guns, but when they saw McLain's badge they lowered their pistols and backed away.

'It's all over,' shouted the lawman. 'Ain't nothing' to see but two corpses. Best go back to your rooms. It's all over.'

'Bar the shooting,' a lisping voice remarked. 'And that's from behind.'

'Leave it off!' McLain shouldered through the crowd. 'Ain't nothin' to see.'

'You leave it off and I'll be the judge,' said the same voice.

McLain veered suddenly to the side, one big hand reaching out to grab a diminutive man dressed in fringed buckskin pants and a bright red shirt.

'You got a big mouth, feller.' The marshal was angry. 'Keep it flappin' an' I might just fill it.'

The man giggled. 'With what?'

'This,' said McLain. And punched his fist into the leering face.

The man flew back as the peace officer let loose his shirt. His nose was pulped back against his cheeks, spreading two wide blobs of crimsoned mucus across his face, joining the mash of his lips to add a fresh splash of colour to his fancy outfit. He hit the wall and slid to the floor. His eyes were closed and as he breathed, frothy bubbles of blood burst from his flattened nostrils.

'He hit Jody,' someone said. 'He punched him!'

'Jody wanted a piece of the action,' snarled Azul. 'He just got a taste. From the peace officer.'

Chapter Nine

Denver faded into the night, a scattering of lights and smell. Both were hidden fast by distance and the rising sun.

Grace complained bitterly at their early departure, but her mother argued her into quiet when Azul explained the nature of the attack and the letter he had found in Levi Brown's room. McLain had got a storekeeper out of bed to restock their supplies, and anything else they might need could be found in Cheyenne: the next stop along their line of travel.

They had left in the quiet hours of the morning, long before the town came awake, and now they were moving parallel to the lines of the Kansas Pacific railroad, heading due north towards the Wyoming border.

The rails shone bright with frost as the sun filtered through the sky-cover of looming cloud. Crystals of ice shone from the metal tracks and the wooden sleepers. The mules plodded forwards in a haze of expelled breath, their hoofs throwing up flutters of dancing frost with each step. Azul rode in front of the wagon, his topcoat buttoned tight, the collar turned up against the chilling wind. Behind him, guiding the team with steady patience, Hope Walls was huddled inside a man's topcoat, her fingers protected by woollen gloves and a knitted scarf wound about her head and neck. Grace wore a close-fitting coat, fur-collared and buttoned in brass. Her hands were thrust inside a fur muff that matched the hat tugged down about her face.

After the initial protests she had fallen into a sulky silence, just bundling up inside her expensive coat and staring aimlessly at the bleak horizon. Her mother kept up a constant stream of chatter – whether to cheer up her daughter or to reassure herself, Azul could not tell. He sensed, though, that both women were preoccupied with the events of the previous night. And once again the doubts crept into his mind: so far someone had spent in excess of four thousand dollars trying to stop the wagon. That was a whole lot of money to chance on hired killers. So, presumably, the prize was worth considerably more. But what was the prize? He doubted that the land titles would justify that kind of expenditure, because they would be registered with lawyers, making it difficult for any robber to take them over unless he had the signature of the women on the papers. But the aim so far seemed to be that both Hope and Grace should die; which had to mean some other motive than simply taking possession of the documents.

But what that motive was, Azul could not guess.

He decided to forget that particular problem in favour of the more immediate difficulties. Like getting the wagon through to Jericho, where – he hoped – the whole thing might be solved.

The sun came through the clouds, lighting up the plains with a sure, golden radiance. Mist rose for a spell, then got melted away under the heat. A bird began singing from the cover of a patch of woodland, its trilling answered by another, then another, until full day dawned, spreading a clear sky streaked through with red over the High Plains.

Azul reined in the grey stallion and waved for the wagon to halt.

'I'm hungry,' he said. 'Let's eat breakfast.'

'Is that wise?' asked the older woman. 'Suppose those men had friends?'

'They had friends,' Azul nodded, grinning as he remembered the Resthouse. 'But I don't think they'll come after us. Besides, we'll spot them easily.'

He pointed back towards the town. The ground was flat, its surface interrupted only by occasional stands of timber and the gleaming rails. To the west the wide band of the South Platte glistened in the early sun, the river's surface dappled by little waves as melting snow from the hills added to its volume, speeding its flow so that the coursing water maintained a constant gurgling, rustling sound. Beyond the river, the high flanks of the Rocky Mountains bulked up from the plain, a massive, impressive barrier. Denver was out of sight, but any pursuit would become clearly visible once the pursuers came within eyes' range: Azul had chosen his spot deliberately.

He built a small fire as the women prepared food, then settled down to eat as the crisp morning air got filled with the savoury odour of frying bacon and sizzling eggs.

A train passed them during the afternoon. A big Baldwin locomotive hauling two carriages and three boxcars. The firemen waved as the great black machine thundered by, and the engineer sounded the whistle, the shrill squeal of sound echoing over the silent landscape. Azul watched the dark line of cars fade away to the north, the reminder bringing all the doubts pouring back into his mind.

If the two women had decided to quit their home for good there was little reason – by his thinking – to cart furniture overland. Why not sell it? And ride the trains north? They could have picked up the Atchison, Topeka and Santa Fe line in Santa Fe, then ridden through to Topeka and the junction with the Kansas Pacific. That would have taken them on to Cheyenne, or Julesburg, or Fort Kearney, where they might have picked up a river boat or a wagon. The river offered the easiest passage, at least as far as Fort Fetterman, and from there they might have covered the last stages by wagon. The journey would have taken longer – thanks to the wide detours of the railroads – but it would have been more comfortable, and considerably safer.

But the two women had chosen the more arduous overland route, travelling by wagon.

The wagon: it always came back to that. The unusually heavy wagon, with its thickened walls and stacked furniture.

Azul turned in the saddle, staring at the vehicle. The mules plodded slowly onwards, chests tight against the traces, the wagon settled low on the springs. Too low, he thought, for the weight of gear inside.

He shrugged, turning away, wondering if his judgement might be wrong. Accustomed to the swift horseback travel of the Apaches, he had little experience of wagons. His father had used a similar vehicle from time to time, but that had been one of the lighter, Mexican-style carts favoured by the Santa Fe traders. Perhaps he was imagining the weight. Perhaps he was misjudging the women's attachment to their belongings, to their personal possessions.

It was an example of his divided blood, his halfbreed background. An Apache warrior owned little more than his clothes, his ponies and his weapons. A lodge might be built from branches and hides, the interior furnished in the same way: from natural materials that were readily available. A *rancheria* might establish more permanent dwelling places, but nothing so fixed that it would require a wagon to transport it. Nor would the owners feel so attached that there was a need for such transportation. Like most Indians, the people of Apacheria were essentially nomadic. They lived in accord with the land, following the seasons that determined the availability of food and clothing and the stuff necessary to home-building. They took their living from the land – as much as they needed; as much as the land gave; and no more – without any need for fixed things. In winter, when the high hills got cold and the living hard, they drifted south. Like the buffalo. If a warrior wanted a bed, he found pine branches and covered them with a blanket. If he wanted something more substantial he killed a buffalo and fashioned a frame from branches, using the sinews of the shaggy beast to provide a couch over which the cured hide could be spread.

Everything was there: in the land. At least until the white men came and began to take it all away.

That was the difference: the white men felt a need for

fixed places. For houses that were built from living timber and honest stone. Places that could not be moved. A need for equally static furniture: chairs, when a man could as easily squat on the ground; tables, when the earth or a hand served just as well; cupboards and wardrobes and trunks to hold his accumulation of possessions, where an Apache would have owned only what he needed – and so had no need for all those containers.

Had Azul been in the position of Hope Walls, he would have given away everything but his basic necessities. Indeed, when he rode away from his *rancheria* he had taken only his weapons, a supply of ammunition, and a single pony.

It was the basic difference between the red and the white peoples: the red wanted no more than a communion with the land that allowed them to live in accord; the whites wanted to own it. *Needed* to own it. Needed to establish dominance over the natural forces of wind and water, summer and winter.

And thus, he reasoned, Hope Walls found it necessary to bring with her those items of her life that roused her memory, assuring her of her place on the earth.

To Azul, that was like carrying a tombstone. But he could – almost – understand the need of the white women.

The weather continued warm and clear, the threat of snow dissipated by a warm wind blowing up from the south. The confrontation of warmth and chill produced rain, so that for two days they moved through a steady drizzle, the hooves of the wagon team clopping soggily over the moist ground.

On the sixth day after leaving Denver they reached Cheyenne.

They were in Wyoming now, their ultimate destination under a month's travel away.

The town bulked up from the prairie much like Denver. The buildings were, at most, two storeys high, and the same concentration of pens and warehouses surrounded the depot of the Kansas Pacific where it joined the terminal of the Union Pacific.

The depot was the busiest part of town, but the Army detachments that might usually have been found there were drafted north as the Sioux and Cheyenne gathered for the spring grazing, and the buffalo hunters had moved south after the herds.

But the depot remained the obvious crossing point for two women heading north with something someone unknown was willing to spend several thousand dollars on getting.

Azul suggested they should camp outside of Cheyenne while he took a mule in and bought supplies.

Grace objected, but once again her mother overrode her arguments and told the halfbreed to go ahead. He unhitched one of the mules and fastened a rope halter about its neck. Then he went down into Cheyenne. The wagon was halted in a stand of liveoaks, the team watered and fed, and both women impressed with the need to keep the Winchesters close at hand. There was nothing more the halfbreed could do; except get the supplies and try to stay clear of trouble.

Cheyenne smelled a little better than Denver, but not much. There were buffalo bones piled around the stockyards and a pair of locomotives shugging greasy steam into the morning air. The centre was cleaner, the wind that had gotten up from the north taking away the worst of the charnel-stink so that only a faint memory remained of the mouldering flesh still attached to the bones. Nor were there any hunters in town, to add their unsavoury odour to the wind: in comparison with Denver, Cheyenne was spring-fresh.

Azul walked the grey stallion down mainstreet, leading the mule behind. He saw a general store and halted both animals. Hope Walls had given him fifty dollars, though he doubted he would need that much – even though he wanted to buy sufficient supplies to take them over the remainder of the journey without another food-stop.

No one took much notice of him as he entered the store, wandering around the displays of meat and the counters of dry goods until he made up his mind exactly what he wanted. Then a grey-haired clerk with a striped apron covering his grubby white shirt came over to take the order. Azul asked for salted bacon, two sides; flour; sugar; coffee; salt. Dough for bread. Dried beef; dried beans; dried fruit; baking soda and corn meal; molasses. Then vinegar, pepper and salt; eggs; rice; and – especially requested by Hope – tea.

'Sounds like you're stockin' fer a siege,' grinned the clerk. 'Or figger to do some huntin'. We got plenty o' Sharps cartridges in stock. You want some?'

Azul shook his head. 'No. Just the food.'

'Where you headin'?' The clerk began to fill the order, speaking as he loaded sacks with the food; making conversation.

'North,' Azul said. 'Up towards Fort Fetterman.'

'Might need shells, then.' The clerk adjusted his half-frame spectacles on his beaky nose. 'Been injun trouble up there. Sioux been hittin' the Army pretty hard.'

'Give me two cartons of ·45, then,' said Azul. 'The Colt and Winchester cross-overs.'

'Sure.' The clerk filled a bag with beans and ambled over to a glass-fronted display case. 'Bastards gotten real uppity of late.'

'Maybe they figure there's too many settlers taking their land,' grunted Azul. 'Reckon it's time they did something about it.'

'Yeah.' The clerk failed to catch the bitterness in the half-breed's voice. 'Stupid bastards. They'll just get killed, which serves 'em right.' He dragged two cases of shells from the cabinet and dropped them into the sack on top of the beans. 'But I heard there's a new feller comin' out this way to back Terry. Man called Custer. Done real well in the Civil War, so I heard. Way I heard it, he should teach the goddamn savages a real lesson.'

'That right?' said Azul.

'Yeah.' The clerk's balding head nodded in vigorous agreement with his own comments. 'Real fire-eater, is Custer. Least, that's what I read.'

'Don't believe everything you read,' murmured Azul. 'Even the biggest fire-eater might have to swallow his words.'

'Not him.' The clerk shook his head. 'Done real good in the war. Youngest goddamn general in the whole Union Army. With him backin', I reckon Terry an' Crook will sort out the whole Sioux nation. Teach them savages a lesson they won't forget.'

'Maybe,' said Azul. 'There been much trouble lately?'

'Like I said,' grunted the clerk, warming even more to his subject, 'They been hitting the Army some. The odd wagon train, too. Been a few settlements wiped out.'

'Which?' asked Azul. 'You got names?'

'Brandon.' The clerk scratched his bald patch. 'That was one. Then there was the Carver trading post. Though that lazy bastard never done much except read fancy books an' get drunk on other people's likker. But they hit Fisherman's Creek, up on the North Platte, an' then Campbell's Settlement.'

'How about a place called Jericho?' Azul asked. 'You got any word on that.'

'Where?' The clerk looked confused.

'Jericho,' Azul repeated. 'Close on the Montana line.'

'Never heard of it.' The clerk shook his head. 'Where is it?'

'Don't worry.' Azul decided to forget about the future in favour of worrying about tomorrow. 'It's not anywhere.'

'Biblical, that name.' The clerk hiked his glasses on to his forehead and puckered up his eyes. 'I recall it from my Bible lessons. Feller smashed the walls down. Feller called Joshua?'

'I don't know,' said Azul. 'Might have been. What do I owe you?'

The clerk looked at the checklist in his hand and began to

scribble sums on a piece of torn bag. 'Thirty seven dollars.'

Azul peeled the notes from the wad Hope had given him: 'Add a couple of big sacks and enough cord to tie them on a mule.'

'Thirty eight. You can have the sacks fer free.'

'Thanks.'

The clerk helped him load the provisions, then watched as the halfbreed slung them over the mule's back. He was surprised when Azul mounted the grey stallion and turned to the south.

'Thought you said you was goin' northwards,' he called. 'Up to Fetterman.'

'Like you heard about that Custer man,' grinned Azul. 'You shouldn't believe everything you hear.'

'What d'you mean?' The clerk scratched his head. 'You know something I don't?'

But Azul was too far down mainstreet, and the clerk was left in doubt. He shrugged and went back inside the store, muttering something about know-it-all hunters. It never occurred to him that the man he had just served might be of interest to Mr Smith, who had slipped him five dollars to keep his eyes open and promised ten more for reliable information. Mr Smith was staying in the Curzon hotel, but when he had spoken to the clerk he had been very definite about the people he wanted: an elderly woman with grey hair and a younger woman, attractive, dark-headed; most likely travelling by wagon, with a fair-haired man hired on as guide. Sure, the hunter had worn a mane of blond hair, but he was on his own – no sign of women with him. The clerk forgot about Azul and went back to his regular chores.

Azul went back to the wagon, riding in slow so that the women would recognise him and not fire on sight. They were pleased to see him return safely. At least Hope was pleased – Grace merely relieved that she was protected again.

They helped him unload the mule and stow the provisions in the wagon. Then Azul got the beast back in harness and they started off again.

They made a wide detour around Cheyenne, swinging over to the west to skirt the town before continuing northwards on a direct line towards Fort Fetterman. Their route took them along the eastern edge of the hills cradling the High Plains, the going slowed by the nature of the terrain. Following the shallow valley of the South Platte had been easy, the land uniformly flat. Now it became more mountainous,the trail winding narrowly along steep-sided rock, or twisting through basins and ravines.

The accident happened as they were thinking about finding a camping site.

They were moving along the downslope of a steep ridge, the upper levels heavy with timber and the last of the snow still visible around the peaks. The trail was formed from some primeval shifting of the rock that had thrust a long ledge out from the side. To the west it was banded by the scarp of the upper slopes; to the east, by a sheer drop, occasionally punctuated by rock slides, that angled down to the bed of a narrow stream. Azul was out in front, letting the grey stallion set its own pace over the uneven ground, about three hundred yards ahead of the wagon. The mules – surer-footed than the horse – were coming on at a brisk walk. As usual, Hope Walls was handling the team, her daughter clutching a carbine and looking bored on the seat beside her mother.

The sun was shifting towards the upper limits of the hills, shedding a reddish glow over the land beneath so that the trees threw shadow across the trail. A flight of ravens passed overhead and a bluejay screamed its strident call as it settled down for the night. High up, Azul heard the snorting challenge of a bighorn ram.

Then a shriek.

He turned, right hand dropping automatically to the stock of his rifle.

The wagon was canted back at an angle over the side of the trail. The rear wheels had slid on a patch of shale slickened by melting snow. Grace was down in front, cursing as she clutched the harness of the two lead mules, trying to drag them onwards as Hope cracked the whip from the drive seat.

The conestoga moved slowly backwards. The mules were straining against the traces, but the weight of the big wagon was negating their efforts, dragging them inexorably back. The wheel spun, throwing a clutter of shale down into the stream. Then it spun loose, the gravel-cleansed rim sharding bright rays of light across the ravine.

Azul turned the grey and urged the part-Arab to a gallop back towards the wagon.

He tugged his rope loose from the saddlehorn and slung a hitch around the tongue of the conestoga, adding the stallion's strength to the power of the mules.

'Get down!' he yelled. 'The whole thing might go over.'

'No!' Obstinately, Hope kept hold of the reins. Went on using the whip.

The loose shale moved. Azul felt his rope stretch tight. Then felt the grey horse begin to slide back, legs stiff, as the bulk of the wagon shifted farther out.

Gravel spilled in a cascading fall, splashing into the stream. The right-hand side of the conestoga struck the rim of the drop, forcing the forward wheel on the same side clear of the trail. The tongue angled down, threatening to lift the rear-most mules off the ground.

'Get off!' he shouted.

'No!' The grey head shook. 'I won't!'

Grace screamed.

Azul shucked the rope clear of the saddlehorn, unwilling to see the grey stallion dragged down with the tilting wagon. He powered clear of the saddle and ran to the rear. The conestoga was tilted over at a crazy angle, the right-hand wheels both clear of the trail, the forward left-hand wheel spinning loose as it came away from the ground. More shale spilled from under the grounded bed.

He seized the one good wheel and tried to turn it forwards

as Grace dug her heels into the soil and fought to drag the mules forwards. Hope was standing up in the seat, still clutching the reins and lashing the whip over the animals' flanks.

The pin connecting the tongue to the forward axle snapped.

Grace fell down screaming as the team surged up the trail.

Hope screamed as the wagon slid backwards.

It canted over, slithering through the shale. At the same time, the grey-haired woman was yanked clear of the seat by the reins wound about her left wrist. She released her grip as her feet quit the jockey-box.

She flew several feet through the air, landing on her face at the side of the trail. The shale gave under her weight and she began to slide down towards the stream in a welter of limbs and petticoats.

'Hold the mules!' Azul yelled at Grace.

Then went over the side after Hope.

He sprang directly on to the slide, jamming his heels into the shifting gravel and riding it down like a tobogganist, oblivious of the wagon that threatened to topple on to him and the sharp splinters of rock that struck his hands and face as he tried to control his downwards motion.

Hope slithered, face down, as far as the stream. Then her legs struck the boulders flanking the watercourse and she stopped. Too fast. A cascade of loose stones pelted her body and she slumped still, partially covered by the shale.

Azul controlled his slide, lifting to his feet so that he was able to run clear before he, too, hit the boulders. He stopped, panting, and ran over to where Hope lay.

The wagon shifted back, then halted, its downwards passage blocked by a narrow ledge. The rear wheels remained on solid ground; the fronts spun loose. Grace went on screaming as she dragged the mules to a halt.

Azul went over to Hope.

She was crumpled against the boulders, her black dress

hiked up about her waist to expose black-stockinged legs that twisted at odd angles. Her feet were clad in short boots, the lower parts twisted round. When he turned her over he saw that her face was torn by the fall, the nose and mouth ripped by the sharp pieces of stone. More blood showed down the front of her dress.

Azul peered up the slope, seeing Grace on hands and knees, staring back.

'Get the rope from the wagon,' he shouted. 'Fix it to the saddlehorn and then throw it down.'

He splashed water over Hope's face as he waited. It didn't revive her, but the blood got washed away. Then the rope curled down the slope. He fashioned a fresh loop and dropped it about his thighs. Picked up the old lady, cradling her body in both arms. It was difficult to keep hold of both her and the lariat, but somehow he managed it.

'All right! Walk the horse forwards. Slowly!'

The rope got tight and he began to walk up the slope, trying hard not to jostle Hope Walls.

The final section was the most difficult, for there he had to negotiate the overhanging bulk of the wagon and the steepest part of the ravine. His feet sank deep into the shale, then came free as he began to clamber over the bare rimrock. Grace let go the stallion when he shouted, and came running back to help him. She reached out for her mother, showing more strength than he had suspected as she helped him ease the old woman on to firm ground.

'Is she all right?'

Azul topped the rise and dragged the lariat clear of his body. The grey horse halted as the rope came clear, moving over to join the patient mules in cropping the grass along the trail.

The halfbreed studied the woman, looking at the exaggerated angulation of her legs. At the ragged mess of her face and hands.

'She's bad hurt,' he murmured, 'but we've not lost Hope yet.'

Chapter Ten

Hope Walls had lost most of the skin from her face and hands. Her legs were broken at the knees and ankles, and her left arm was dislocated. Azul sprung the arm back in place, but after that the most he could do was see her wrapped up in blankets with crude splints on her legs and a fire built up to keep her warm.

Grace prepared a broth from their supplies as the half-breed dragged blankets from the wagon to make a bed on the side of the trail.

'They'll have a doctor in Cheyenne,' he said. 'I'll ride back an' fetch him.'

'The hell you will!' The voice was faint, cloaked with pain. But still firm. 'You go back there, an' you won't just bring a doctor. You'll bring every goddamn bounty hunter running fast on your tail.'

'Momma!' Grace set the pans down as she launched herself across the rough ground. 'You need a doctor.'

'At the next place we stop,' said Hope. 'Not here. Not from Cheyenne. Like Azul said – that's the most likely place they'll look for us. You just keep me comfortable an' push on. Got some whisky in the wagon. That'll fend off the hurts.'

'The wagon's half-way over the road, momma. I don't know if we can save it.'

'Oh, Jesus!' Hope's eyes closed for a moment. Then opened wide as she stared at her daughter. 'You have to save it! You know that.'

'I'll do my best, momma.' Grace looked at Azul, and for the first time the halfbreed saw genuine appeal there. 'Me and Mr Gunn . . . Azul, that is . . . Won't we?'

He nodded. 'Sure. But we still need a doctor.'

'No.' Hope tried to shake her head. 'Don't go back to Cheyenne. Just get the wagon back on the trail and put me inside. Promise me.'

'You'll die,' said Azul, bluntly. 'Gangrene'll set in. Even if it don't, you'll never walk straight again. Never walk again, more like.'

'Five hundred dollars extra.' Hope raised a bandaged hand. 'That makes it a thousand if you get the wagon through to Jericho.'

'What about you?' The halfbreed felt genuine concern; born of respect for the old woman. 'You want to die along the way?'

'Just get the wagon through to my brother,' muttered Hope, her voice fading. 'That an' my daughter. If you hafta bury me, try to make it in Jericho. I'd like that.'

'You're crazy,' grunted Azul. 'But you're still the boss.'

The Apache side of his nature appreciated her determination. Applauded it, even. He knew enough about wounds to recognise the fact that her legs were gone for good. At best, a doctor might patch her together as a cripple, or ease her dying; but he could never mend her: she was too badly smashed for that. He fetched the whisky bottle from the wagon and poured a generous measure into a coffee mug.

The spirit burned her lips as she swallowed, but it went some way to easing the pain. She coughed, tears running down her face as the movement racked her damaged flesh.

'More. I've not drunk whisky since my husband died.'

Azul filled the mug again. 'Thanks,' said Hope when she finished it. 'I feel better now. Leave me to sleep. We'll shift the wagon in the morning.'

Grace spoke as her mother's head slumped back against the blanket covering the frame bed Azul had built: 'We have to bring a doctor.'

'I forbid it!' Hope opened her eyes just long enough to speak. 'You will do as I say.'

'Yeah,' nodded Azul. 'Yes, ma'am.'

'Good.' The grey head sank back and the gallant old lady let sleep overtake her mind.

Morning dawned clear and bright. Azul got the fire started up again and had coffee brewing before Grace woke. He checked Hope, finding her locked fast in the unconsciousness produced as a guard against shock and pain. Her face, under its mask of drying blood, was thinner than he remembered, and sweat beaded the ravaged flesh. She moaned softly, each sound bursting tiny bubbles of frothy, bloodstained matter from her nostrils. He moistened a cloth and wiped her face as gently as if she were a child.

'What are you doing?'

Grace sat up, glaring at him. He said: 'Looking after your mother.'

'I'll do that.' She thrust her blanket aside and climbed to her feet. 'Leave her alone.'

Azul shrugged and tossed the cloth at the daughter. Grace started cursing as her fluttering hands lost the rag. Azul went over to the wagon.

'See to her, then. I'll try an' get this thing back on the road.'

Grace pouted and began to wipe her mother's face afresh. Azul studied the wagon, then went to feed the mules and his own horse.

'I thought you were checking the wagon,' said Grace.

'You want me to lift it singlehanded?' The halfbreed felt anger begin to swell inside him. 'I'll need a strong team to shift the thing.'

Grace emitted a sound like an angry heifer; but settled down to preparing breakfast.

Azul went back to studying the conestoga.

After a while he wandered off into the trees and began to cut branches with an axe taken from the wagon's toolbox. He cut numerous branches and one tall young pine, from which he trimmed the limbs. The cutting and the hard labour of transferring the branches to the lower part of the trail took up most of the day. It was late afternoon before he had everything in place.

There was a spare pin in the toolbox, so he got the tongue of the wagon fixed back to the main body and put the mules back in the harness. Then he piled the brushwood under the forwards wheels, providing as firm a base as he could. After that he climbed down on to the ledge supporting the right-hand rear wheel and poked the pole beneath the body. He got the wood settled in under the bed of the wagon and then built a small cairn of stones up high enough that it would provide a fulcrum.

By the time he was finished the sun was going down again.

He checked Hope Walls and washed quickly in the water from the barrel slung alongside the conestoga.

Grace asked, 'Well? Are you going to shift the thing? Or do we go back to Cheyenne?'

Azul shook his head. 'Your mother said not to. She hired me, so I do what she says.'

'She won't do anything if you don't get us moving.' Grace's pretty face got screwed up with anger. Or maybe fear. 'She needs a doctor. Bad.'

'I know that,' grunted the halfbreed. 'But she gave orders. I'll respect them.'

'I suppose you always do,' snapped Grace. 'Suppose I gave you a fresh set?'

'I'd ignore them,' rasped Azul. 'Your mother said what she wanted: I'm going to do it.'

It was Chiricahua obstinacy coming out. That and the firm belief that dying friends – and he thought of Hope Walls as both dying and a friend – had the right to determine their own way out of the world.

There is little a man can hope for in life except his passage through it and the way in which he leaves it. Sees-Both-Ways, the Chiricahua shaman had told him that. And the philosophy was supported by his father and old Sees-The-Fox. *The manner of his going is all that is left him in the end. He can die well, or badly. Only the ones beyond judge that, after a man has travelled the Star Road. There, they decide. So the best you can do for someone about to take that path is to leave them to take their own way along the road.*

'You mean you'll leave her die?' snapped Grace. 'Just let her rot away?'

'No.' Azul shook his head. 'I mean I'll do what she told me.'

'Wouldn't make much difference if you didn't.' Hope woke up, staring through pain-bleared eyes at her daughter and the halfbreed. 'I know I'm dying. Ain't really unexpected at my age. Nor unexpected to give some last requests. Like not bringing a doctor out. An' getting the wagon through to Jericho. You do that an' I'll pass over happy.'

'Momma! You don't know what you're saying.' Grace began to wipe the old woman's face. 'You're fevered.'

'I'm hurting, that's all,' said Hope. 'I got bust up pretty bad on that fall. Stupid thing! I should've known better. Fact remains, though: I'm dying. What I want now is to get to Jericho. Maybe see Joshua one last time. That's all I want.'

She ignored her weeping daughter, looking instead at Azul. 'Will you promise me that?'

'I'll do the best I can,' said the halfbreed. 'I can't promise more.'

'That's good enough for me,' murmured Hope Walls. 'You done pretty good so far. Now keep it up.'

'Yeah.' Azul climbed to his feet. 'I'll do my best.'

He walked away, leaving Grace crying on her mother's shoulder as if she was the hurt one, and began to prepare food. While it was heating he took the mules out of the traces and hobbled them on a tether line. Then he spread his bedroll over the cold ground and saw to his horse.

Hope Walls passed out again before the food was ready, so Azul and Grace ate in resentful silence before spooning broth into the old lady's mouth.

They managed to get a good deal inside her before she

closed her ragged lips and shut her eyes. So they cleaned her face again and settled the blankets about her body. Azul built the fire up higher and then climbed inside his own blankets.

'Aren't you going to keep guard?' asked Grace, maliciously. 'Isn't that what you're paid for?'

'Don't worry,' grunted Azul. 'I'll look after you. Now shut your mouth. In case someone hears it.'

'You bastard!' Grace's voice was bitter. 'You callous halfbreed bastard. My mother's dying over there.'

'And moving her won't do much good,' muttered Azul. 'You heard what she wanted.'

Grace snorted and turned her back, dragging the blankets up to her chin. Azul stretched out, staring at the sky. The night was clear and cool, faint traces of cloud drifting across the heavens so the panorama of stars seemed to flicker on and off, like distant lights. An owl hooted, and from the far side of the ravine a nightjar called. Off to the north he heard a wolf howl, the eerie cry answered by another, then a third. He looked at the wagon, then at the silent shape of Hope Walls. Then he closed his eyes and fell asleep.

By morning, the old woman was locked in the grip of a fever. Sweat drenched her body and she mumbled incoherently, her body twitching as spasms of pain racked her nerves. Grace did what she could to make her mother more comfortable, ignoring Azul except when he spoke directly to her.

The halfbreed made breakfast himself, eating his portion hurriedly, then leaving the plates for Grace to clean. He went over to the wagon, checking his preparations.

When he was satisfied, he harnessed the team and went over to Grace. 'You'll have to handle the mules. Can you do that?'

Grace shrugged. 'I don't know. I've never driven mules before.'

'Now's a good time to learn,' grunted Azul. 'Listen.' He

explained what he wanted her to do.

Grace climbed warily on to the canted seat, taking the reins in her left hand and the whip in her right. Azul clambered down the slope to the ledge, grasping the pine pole in both hands, his fingers interlaced above the wood.

'Now!' he yelled. 'Whip them up!'

Grace shouted, cracking the whip inexpertly over the animals. The mules, stung by the leather, surged forwards. Azul dragged down on the pole, fighting to lift the wagon back on an even keel where the wheels would grip enough to afford purchase.

The conestoga was too heavy.

'Hold it!' Azul let go the pole. 'Set the brake.'

He climbed back on the trail and waved Grace down from the seat.

'We'll have to unload.'

'What?' She sounded oddly nervous. 'That will take hours.'

'It's the only way. This thing's too heavy right now.'

Grace agreed with reluctance, and they began to empty the wagon. The furniture was heavier than Azul had expected, its removal made more difficult by the need to unload from the side, but they managed to get it all off. By which time the morning had passed and they were both tired and hungry.

Grace got a meal scraped together and checked her mother. Hope was calmer now, though still feverish. The wounds on her hands and face were drying, but her features seemed sunken in: she appeared smaller, almost withered. Azul saw that she was dying, and wondered how long her fierce spirit would hold on to life.

'Let's try it again.'

Grace nodded without speaking, and got back on the wagon.

'Now!'

As the whip cracked, Azul threw all his weight against the pole.

The wagon shifted a little.

The mules sensed the movement and strained against the harness. The conestoga moved forwards an inch or so, the bottom scraping along the edge of the drop. Loose shale spilled out around the halfbreed and he shouted for Grace to keep going. The forward wheels dug into the brushwood, splintering branches as weight settled on the pine knots. Azul threw himself across the pole, balancing on his stomach and bouncing up and down in an attempt to provide the extra leverage needed.

The wagon moved further, its motion threatening to dislodge the pole from its fulcrum and spill the halfbreed out into the ravine. He yelled for Grace to stop. Then cut more wood which he piled under the raised rear wheel.

They tried again.

The conestoga shifted several feet forwards, dragging the pole clear of the stones so that Azul was forced to jump away as rocks and gravel tumbled down the slope. It took another hour to rebuild the cairn and get the pole back in place, with the brushwood stacked in new positions.

Then they resumed their efforts.

The front wheels lurched heavily on to the trail. Azul shouted at Grace to keep driving the team forwards, and let go the pole. He ducked down, moving back along the ledge until he was directly beneath the wagon. He noticed that a section of wood along the right-hand frame was split, the colour of the break shining oddly. He decided to check it later, and positioned himself beneath the rear wheel.

'Now!'

Once again the mules stamped forwards, but this time there were three wheels on relatively firm bases. And the halfbreed was under the wagon, heaving up in unison with the team. Azul's strength and the forward motion of the animals lifted the wagon to the horizontal.

The right-hand rear wheel spun loose from the brushwood. Pieces of timber scattered about Azul. His body screamed as he braced a shoulder under the edge of the bed and concentrated on lifting the vehicle over the rim.

It lurched. And he felt the wheel touch his back, falling to his knees as the entire body of the conestoga passed above his head. Sweat ran down his face. His shoulder was a numb ache, the left arm devoid of feeling, and throbbing pain ran through his legs and chest.

But the wagon was back on the trail: he pushed to his feet and hauled himself up behind it.

'We did it!' Grace came running back. 'We saved it.'

'Yeah.' Azul slumped to the ground, massaging his shoulder. Slowly, like water leaking through a worn-out canteen, feeling returned to his arm and hand. He flexed the arm, wincing as the muscles were brought into play. 'Give me a shot of that whisky.'

Grace located the bottle and passed it to him. Azul tilted the neck, taking a long, deep swallow. The alcohol dulled the aches in his body, providing him with a rush of fast-used energy. He passed the bottle back.

'There's a strut got broken. I'll take a look before we load up again.'

He rolled over on hands and knees and crawled under the wagon. The axles were sound and most of the bed was still firm, only the split timber he had seen earlier showing any damage. He peered at it.

The wood was only marginally damaged, a splintered strip torn away when the conestoga slid off the trail. It was nothing serious: certainly nothing that need halt their journey. Except for the one thing: the curious shine from inside the wood. He peeled the splinters away and drew his Bowie knife, probing into the crack.

The Bowie struck metal. Azul grunted in surprise, then carved a wider chunk of wood clear. Scraped the knife along the length of the split.

And cursed.

He crawled clear of the vehicle and eased to his feet. Grace came around the far side with a Winchester in her hands. The hammer was cocked and she suddenly looked like she knew how to use the carbine.

'Silver!' Azul's voice was a low, animal snarl. 'You goddamn bitches fooled me into bringing a silver wagon north.'

'That's right.' Grace's lovely face was a mixture of fear and smug approval of their trickery. 'It's everything we could take from the mine. That and the deeds. That part was true.'

'The whole wagon?' Azul was amazed. 'Is that why it's so heavy?'

Grace nodded. 'Sure. All the timbers are hollowed out. We got that done in Galenas. The furniture, too. Then we filled the spaces up with silver. Momma promised Uncle Joshua that. It buys us a stake in his town.'

'And it's why those hired guns been waiting for you,' rasped Azul. 'Because someone knows about the wagon?'

'I guess.' Grace smiled without shifting her aim. 'Real lucky for us that we met you.'

'Yeah.' Azul's voice was rueful. 'But why this way? Why not just sell up and transfer the money to a bank?'

'From Mexico?' Grace sounded scornful. 'If we'd done that, the government would've taken a cut. Border tax, or something like that.'

Azul shrugged. Winced as his shoulder moved, and began to rub his arm. 'You could've hired people to fetch you north. The border's not fenced off.'

'You should know,' said Grace sarcastically. 'You should also know that those kind of people would take the silver.'

'Like me?' Azul went of rubbing his arm.

'Like you.' Grace nodded. 'The only reason you helped us was because momma offered you five hundred dollars. I know what men are like.'

'You know what the ones you've met are like,' grunted Azul. 'And it's a thousand dollars now.'

Grace looked surprised. 'That was before you knew. Now you'll just try to take it all.'

'I gave my word.' Azul's voice got flat and cold. 'That's not a thing I do easy. I made a promise: I'll see it through.'

'I don't believe you.' Grace stared at him, still holding the carbine on his belly. 'I don't trust you.'

Azul rubbed some more at his arm, grimacing as he massaged the stiff muscles. Then he powered sideways, grabbing hold of the wagon wheel to provide a base for the kick he directed at the woman.

The Winchester blasted a shot through the trees on the far side of the ravine as his right foot slammed against the barrel. His left struck Grace on the hip, pitching her off balance so that her hands flew loose from the gun.

Azul dropped to the ground, ignoring the pain in his left side as he rolled over, fetching up on his knees beside the sprawled woman. He grabbed the front of her woollen coat and hauled her to a sitting position as his right hand swung down to swipe across her cheek. Grace's face went white, then red, where his open hand landed. He swung back, landing the reverse of his hand on her left cheek. Her head rocked sideways; he slapped her twice more. Very hard. Tears sprang from her eyes, messing the shadow and the powder.

'You bitch!' He let go of her coat, letting her fall back against the hard earth. 'What did you have figured out? Kill me? Or hold a gun on me all the way to Jericho?'

'I don't know.' Grace turned on her side, rubbing her hands against her cheeks. 'All I know is, momma's dying and I want to get to Uncle Josh.'

'Like I said,' grunted Azul, 'I gave my word on that. I ain't interested in your silver. I got promised a thousand dollars, an' that's enough for me. Now quit weeping and help me load the wagon.'

'You mean you'll go on?' Grace brushed at her face. 'You'll still take us through?'

'I gave my word,' Azul repeated. 'Yeah.'

They got the silver-filled furniture back on the wagon and lashed it all in place. Then they fixed Hope a bed in the back and Azul hitched the grey stallion behind the conestoga while Grace settled beside her mother. The halfbreed got the mules moving as night came down, choosing to make the fastest time possible to the next settlement. And hope they could find a doctor for the dying woman.

'Do you think she'll make it?' asked Grace, humbler now. 'Or will she die?'

'She's got a lot of spirit,' said Azul, 'but she's also got two broken knees. All I can do is try to bury her heart where she wanted.'

Chapter Eleven

They moved slowly, hampered by darkness and the difficult trail. At dawn Azul called a halt, and they fed Hope some broth. The old woman was out of her delirium now, but not clear of the fever that, together with the shock of her injuries, had weakened her natural resources to the point where she hung precariously between life and death.

Azul stopped again at noon and twilight, then pushed on down the descending slope to the rolling grasslands of the Wyoming plain. The going was easier here, the rock giving way to the flatlands with a high, bright moon to light their path. He drove through the night, halting again at dawn just long enough to rest the team and get some food inside Hope.

The sun was still burning the dew from the plain when they saw the settlement.

It consisted of no more than a dozen houses built around the low profile of a trading post. A timber fence surrounded the complex, itself flanked by teepees, with a wide gate opening to the south. The buildings were of solid wood and clay construction, each one roofed with turf, the fronts protected by low porches and the windows kept to a minimum. To one side of the stockade there was a corral and a smithy. Half the houses were deserted.

Azul steered in through the gate and halted the wagon outside the trading post. Grace looked round nervously as he climbed down from the seat, eyeing the Indians who clustered around, holding up blankets and buffalo hides as they urged her to buy.

'Stay there,' ordered Azul. 'If you get any trouble, shout.'

He went into the post.

It was cool and dark inside, not yet warmed by the spring sun, but not so cold that anyone had bothered to light the two big stoves set at the centre of the room. There was a plank bar resting on barrels down the right-hand wall and two wide trestle tables at the far end. A scattering of round tables and hand-made seats provided the only other furniture, set out before the bar. A separate counter of pine and brick flanked the left-hand wall, its surface covered with trade goods.

A bored-looking man with long, greasy hair came out from behind a display of harness. His face was sallow and bearded. He wore a dirty white shirt and a fancy vest with the chain of a fob watch strung over his ample belly. The bottom half of a striped suit covered his legs and his feet shuffled in the dust as he dragged his moccasins over to the bar.

'What you lookin' for, mister? Buyin' or drinkin'?'

'A doctor.' Azul swatted an interested fly clear of his mouth. 'You got one?'

'I sell likker an' trade goods, friend.' The man shrugged, going behind the bar to pour himself a generous measure of near-transparent whisky. 'I ain't in the medical profession.'

'Give me a whisky,' Azul said.

It came out of a bottle without a label into a clay mug. There was sediment on the bottom and no colour to hide the view. When Azul sipped it, the taste came close to burning his lips.

'Two cents,' grunted the trader. 'Sell you a whole bottle fer fifty.'

'Be cheaper to buy some shells,' gasped the halfbreed. 'They'd kill me quicker.'

'I got shells, too.' The man filled his own glass to the brim, then added a measure to Azul's mug. 'On the house.'

'Thanks.' Azul took a deep breath and forced more of the home-brew down his throat. 'But I still need a doctor.'

'We don't have no doctor. You don't like my likker?'

Azul shook his head. 'I tasted better.'

'Yeah.' The barkeep sighed, wiping a dirty hand over his beard. 'So've I. Trouble is I can't get no decent stuff in here since troubles started. So I make my own.'

'What troubles?' Azul asked. 'Apart from poisoning folks.'

'Injun trouble is what.' The man lifted the mug again, but Azul raised his pot in time to avoid a refill. 'Sioux an' Cheyenne been actin' up lately. Figure there's too many settlers comin' to the Black Hills lookin' fer gold. Figure the Pa-ha-sa-pha belongs to them, so they ain't partial to whites movin' in. Shit! I used to have a nice little post here before that bastard Custer began shootin' his mouth off. I reckon he just wants to start a rush so he can lead a few squadrons of cavalry against the injuns an' win hisself a big victory. Then he'll get back to bein' a general again. Like he was in the Civil War. You ever see him?'

Azul shook his head.

'Skinny guy with fancy hair.' The barkeep spat on the floor. 'More or less the same colour as your'n. But wavy. Wears real fancy uniforms; an' traipses around with his wife an' kin like he owns the country. I saw him take his hat off once.' He leaned over the counter, winking. 'Bastard was damn' near bald on top o' those fancy locks.'

'I still want a doctor,' said Azul. 'There's a hurt old woman outside. She's got both legs broke an' needs attention.'

'Well, shit!' The trader put his glass down. 'Why didn't you say that right off? We ain't got no regular doctor here, but we got a feller does wonders with hurt horses. He'll fix her. Better'n a real doctor, I reckon.'

'Where is he?' Azul demanded.

The barkeep winked and shuffled out from behind the counter. 'Wait there, friend.'

Azul waited as the man slid through the dust to the end of the trading post and opened a door. He shouted through the outbuildings.

'Murray! Doc Murray! Get up, you lazy bastard! I got you a customer.'

He shuffled back. 'Doc Murray ain't much to look at, but he works damn' good with bones.'

The door opened and a short man came through. He was dressed in a dove grey Eastern-style suit, his grey hair topped by a narrow-brimmed derby. He looked to be about sixty years old, with silvery beard-stubble covering his cheeks and eyes reddened by liquor. He carried a formal black bag in his left hand, and his right held a whisky glass.

'What's the trouble, Mac?' His voice was thick. 'Who wants me?'

'This feller,' said Mac, pointing to Azul. 'Seems like he's got a lady with busted legs.'

'A lady, eh?' The grey-haired man emptied his glass and set it down on one of the trestle tables. 'Bring her in, my friend. Bring her in and let me attend her. A lady will make a pleasant change from cows. Or mares.'

Azul watched the ageing doctor for a moment, then went to fetch Hope Walls from the wagon: even a drunken practitioner was better than none.

He called for Grace to help him, and together they slid the old woman clear of the wagon, carrying her slowly – carefully – inside. Murray and the barkeep had got a table cleared and a fairly clean sheet spread over the surface. There was a bowl of hot water steaming at one end, and the drunken doctor was opening his medical valise at the other. They settled Hope on the sheet.

Then Grace smelled Murray's breath as he moved past her and said, 'I'm not letting a drunk tend my mother.'

'Madam,' Murray answered, 'I may enjoy a fondness for alcohol, but I remain the only doctor between here and Fort Fetterman. You are thus faced with two choices: to allow me the privilege of tending your mother, or to attempt to reach the fort and give her over into the care of some Army butcher. Which would you prefer?'

'We'll trust you, doc,' said Azul. 'On the understanding that you get paid for your work.'

'And how would you calculate that, my friend?' Murray asked. 'From the look of this lady, she might well die should you choose to attempt the arduous journey to Fetterman.'

'What do you charge for a busted leg?' said Azul. 'At going rates?'

'Twenty dollars.' Murray answered fast. 'Thirty if it's complicated.'

'Fine.' Azul nodded, grinning without showing any mirth. 'She's got two broken legs, so we'll pay you forty dollars. Mess it up an' I'll kill you.'

Murray gulped and the barkeep began to hurry over to the counter. Azul drew the Colt and said, 'Don't run away. We might need you.' The barkeep came back.

Doc Murray took the splints Azul had made off of Hope's legs and winced. He worked silently – his drunkenness appeared to be lost under the urgent pressure of his work – and he bound her limbs with clean bandages and fresh splints.

When he finished he said, 'She needs a better doctor than I can be. Needs a real specialist and more medical supplies than I got. The nearest place you'll find the specialist is St Louis. The nearest place you'll find the supplies is Fort Fetterman.'

Grace clapped both hands over her mouth and began to weep.

Azul asked, 'If we take her to Fetterman is there a chance she might live?'

Murray shook his head. 'The Army doctor might stop the gangrene for a while, but I don't think he could halt the thing. At best he could only slow it up. Maybe amputate her legs. She's too far gone for anything else.'

'We must go to St Louis!' Grace took her hands away from her tear-stained face. 'We must!'

Murray shook his head again. 'She'll be dead before you get there. Your best chance is to head on to Fetterman.'

Grace produced a handkerchief and began dabbing at her eyes.

She stood up: 'Thank you, doctor. We'll take my mother to Fort Fetterman as quickly as possible. Isn't that right, Azul?'

'Yeah.' Azul stood up. 'We'll do that.'

Mac and Murray helped them carry Hope back to the wagon, then Grace paid the doctor for his services and they moved north.

When they reached Fort Fetterman the Army doctor took one look at Hope Walls and decided that the only way to save her life was by amputating both legs.

He explained that to Azul and Grace; and left it to them to explain it to Hope.

'No!' Her voice was firm for an old lady with disease creeping through her body. 'I want to die whole. All my parts in place. I don't want no one cutting off my legs.'

'It could save your life, momma.' Grace began to weep. 'Think about that.'

'I thought about it,' said Hope. 'While you was hauling me here. I thought about it when Azul dragged me up from that goddamn ravine. And then I thought about it some more along the way.'

'Momma, you don't know what you're saying,' Grace wailed. 'You'll die.'

'I'll die anyway,' said Hope. 'Besides, if that Army doctor cuts my legs off, I'll be held up here until the stumps heal.'

Her faded face got thinner still, and she struggled for breath even as she smiled. 'I'd sooner chance my life on reaching Jericho an' get buried there.'

She turned away from her daughter to stare at Azul: 'You made me a promise. Does it still hold?'

'Sure.' The halfbreed nodded. 'I'll do what you paid me for.'

'Can't ask more than that,' whispered the old woman. 'Thanks.'

The Army doctor gave them a small supply of medicines that would ease the pain spreading through the old woman's legs. There was nothing anyone could do to halt the contagion creeping up from the broken limbs, except the medications prescribed to ease the pain.

Azul and Grace fed them into her each day as they tracked slowly north out of Fort Fetterman.

The halfbreed kept the wagon down to a slow pace, so as to make the going easier. Which was not difficult over the undulating Wyoming plains.

They rode steadily north, heading directly for the border with Montana. Following the course outlined by the dying woman in the back of the wagon. Azul said nothing more about the deception both women had worked on him, nothing more about the silver-loaded weight of the vehicle and its furniture.

He simply concentrated on the fulfilment of his task: on getting them through the hostile territory to Jericho.

His determination impressed itself on Grace and she complained less, taking her turn with the mules and willingly preparing food each time they halted. The open dislike she had shown him since the start of the journey faded to a strange neutrality. He could not think that they had become friends, for the beautiful woman remained aloof, withdrawn, but the enmity was gone from their relationship, replaced by a shared purpose.

They took turns tending Hope whilst standing watch, for Azul was concerned by the reports of Indian activity. They were now a good three hundred miles from their meeting with the southern Cheyenne and the halfbreed wondered if the influence of the buffalo-bonneted warrior extended so far. The Indian had known of Jericho – that had been clear from the amusement the name produced – but his tribe were based on the High Plains of Colorado, while their current route was taking them through the lands of the northern Cheyenne and the Sioux. It was possible that the Plains Indians had a system of communications similar to the methods used by the Apache, who utilised mirrors to flash messages from hill to hill or signal fires, or swift riders. From time to time Azul had seen signal smoke drifting across the sky, but he had no way of reading the messages contained therein; no way of knowing if the smoke was a warning or a password. So each time they stopped, he or Grace kept watch.

The Army doctor had provided them with a supply of clean bandages in addition to the medical stuff, and they changed Hope's dressings at regular intervals. The old woman was eased some by the drugs, but the contamination of her broken legs spread inexorably. Her ankles were swollen, the flesh puffy and red, the inflammation darkening around the edges of the break. Conversely, her knees appeared withered, the flesh sunken in so that it outlined the bones, hugging close to the splintered ends. The wounds gave off a sickly smell, staining the bandages with discharged pus so that it was necessary to wash them thoroughly each time they came upon a stream or waterhole. Hope, however, remained cheerful when she was awake, asking for the morphine the doctor had provided only when the pain became too great to bear.

After a few days travelling, the discolouration was spread all the way up to her lower legs, and her toe nails began to drop off. Then it spread above her knees, creeping slowly closer to her thighs.

Azul did his best to speed their journey without disturbing the dying woman. He rose before sun-up each morning and got their fire going again. Grace aided him without complaint, no longer making any pretence at modesty or decorum, but washing in whatever water was available while the halfbreed tended the horses, keeping a discreet distance from the half-naked woman. She had given up the fancy dresses worn at the start of the long trek, and now wore simple outfits for days on end. Her hair was no longer the teased and coiffured artifice Azul had seen at the beginning, but drawn back from her face with a plain blue ribbon. If anything, it made her more attractive, adding an element of simplicity to her sensual features.

They halted only when it was absolutely necessary. To rest the animals or sleep or eat. In between, they pushed on, from sunrise to sunset; grabbing a few hours of rest before starting again by the light of the moon.

They were heading along the line of the old Bozeman trail, their path marked by the tracks of the myriad wagons that had gone before, heading up towards Idaho and the silver strikes around Virginia City. They crossed the southern swing of the Powder river, where a small settlement gave them shelter for the night and another doctor examined Hope's legs. He, too, pronounced her close to death, but did what he could to ease her parting, selling them fresh medical supplies before they moved out.

'I guess I'm a burden,' said Hope, during one of her less frequent moments of coherence. 'Insisting on heading for pastures new.'

Azul grinned as he bound the splints in place.

'Not really.' He fastened the bandages tight. 'But you'll sure have postures new.'

Hope Walls laughed and went to sleep.

Chapter Twelve

Beyond the Powder river the country broke up into an alternation of hills and high meadows. Rolling grasslands gave way to timber-studded ravines. The weather shifted like a woman choosing a suitable dress: a rainy morning gave way to a sunny afternoon; one day was filled with grey clouds and drifting drizzle, the next with sunshine. Twice they waited out storms, watching the lightning dance over the hills, seeing tall pines tumble as the forked tongues of sky-borne electricity shattered the trunks, the smell of burning lost beneath the torrents of rain. Then the clouds would get blown away by the north wind and the sky would clear to an azure blue that was streaked with drifting mounds of pure white.

The country got a fresh smell. A smell of grass and budding trees. Birds sang, and the animals that had slept through the winter woke up and came looking for food.

Wolf packs kept both Azul and Grace awake for three nights, scenting the easy prey of the mules. The halfbreed shot two lobos before the packs ran away in search of easier pickings. And once he emptied his rifle into a bear that had decided the mules might be tasty fare after the winter's hibernation.

And then they came to Jericho.

The town was spread along a wide valley that ran on a curving line from east to west. The upper slopes were thick with burgeoning pine and a stream burst clear of the northern rim to spill its water down along the belly of the bottomlands. The houses were built on the northern side, huddled up against the downslope where they were protected from the wind.

There were around thirty houses. Coming out from the timber of the southern slope, Azul picked out a plank bridge over the stream and the usual selection of frontier dwellings: a saloon; a livery stable; an eating house; a general store; a saddlery. The rest were residential buildings.

The odd thing was that smoke lifted only from the single building higher than one storey. The others were silent, the smoke coming from the two-tiered building with the gold-lettered sign across the front, announcing it as the Jericho Palace Hotel.

There were no horses on the street. Nor any people. No smoke rose from the houses built up the slope. There was no movement.

Instead, there was a curiously dead feeling: as though the town was empty; devoid of life.

Azul reined the mules to a halt and turned to Grace Walls.

'Stay here,' he said, 'while I check it out.'

Grace nodded and the halfbreed jumped clear of the wagon, going to the rear to unhitch the grey stallion. He mounted and drew his rifle from the saddle boot. Then heeled the big horse past the wagon on to the downwards trail.

The hoofs rang loud on the planking of the bridge. Louder still as they echoed against the frontages of the buildings. No one appeared on the porches and sidewalks. The windows were open, the shutters drawn back. A random breeze rattled the batwings of the saloon, but no one came out to watch the solitary rider.

Azul reined in outside the hotel.

He hitched the grey stallion to the post and climbed the steps on to the porch. Dust blew thick around his moccasins. More fell from the door as he pushed it open.

There was a vestibule with glass panels and a row of coat

hooks. Beyond that, a door that opened on a small room flanked by chairs. The chairs were thick with dust; like the carpet. And the curtains over the windows.

The desk at the left-hand side of the room was clean. The mahogany surface shone bright; the bell was polished; the register immaculate.

Azul punched the bell-push.

Clapper rang on shining dome. The sound was loud in the quiet.

A man came out from the small office behind the desk. He was a tall man, a few inches higher than Azul. He wore a black suit with a watch chain spanning the sunken gap of his stomach. His hair was white: like snow. It matched the colour of his moustache and the immaculate gleam of his shirt. He reached up to check the knot of his string tie, then turned the register so that it faced the halfbreed.

'Welcome, sir.' He shoved a quill pen set in an obsidian holder across the desk. 'You want a room?'

'That and information,' said Azul. 'Where do I find Joshua Walls?'

The tall man chuckled. 'You speak to him, sir. I am Joshua Walls.'

Azul left the pen in the holder.

'I got your sister an' your niece in a wagon up on the ridge. Hope is bad hurt. You got a doctor here?'

Joshua chuckled. 'I have everything here. I own this town. I do as I want. Bring them to me. I shall see them looked after.'

Azul nodded. 'Hope is real bad. She's got two busted legs with gangrene spreading. Can you get someone to fix that?'

'Bring her to me,' said Joshua. 'All will be well. Did she bring the silver?'

'Yeah.' Azul wondered about the lanky man. 'Sure.'

'Good. Now we can start to build again.'

'I'll go fetch her then,' said the halfbreed. 'Best get that doctor here fast.'

He went out and mounted the grey stallion, urging the horse to a fast gallop up the ridge. He tethered the animal behind the wagon and took the reins of the mule team from Grace.

The dark-haired woman climbed to the back and began talking to her mother.

'We've reached Jericho, momma. Uncle Josh is getting a bed ready. Azul says there's a doctor coming, so you'll be all right. Don't that sound good, momma?'

All Hope Walls did was moan as the conestoga bucked its way down the narrow trail into Jericho.

Azul halted the wagon outside the hotel and set the brake. Joshua and Grace helped him carry the old woman inside the hotel. Then Joshua took a key from the set behind his desk and led the way down the ground-floor corridor.

'She'll be real comfortable in here. Best room I got. Bridal suite, really. Complete with a drawing room an' its own bathroom. Finest I can offer, though nothing's too good for my sister.'

The bed was thick with dust and mice droppings. Grace opened her mouth to protest, but Azul waved her quiet. He lifted the counterpane clear and tossed it aside. The sheets were mildewed, and as they set Hope down, a dark blur of cockroaches ran across the lower sheet.

'No finer room to be found this side of Denver,' crowed Joshua. 'I heard they got some reasonable hotels in Cheyenne, an' suchlike places, but there are few to compare with the Jericho Palace.'

'You're right,' said Azul. 'Now why don't you fix us a meal while we get your sister bedded down?'

'Yes. An excellent suggestion.' Joshua bowed his way from the room. 'I shall organise a meal fit for an emperor. Fit for the friends of my beloved sister.'

The door swung closed behind him and Grace turned to face Azul.

'He's mad,' she said. 'My Uncle Josh is raving mad.'

'Seems that way,' Azul agreed. 'And best I can tell, this town is empty.'

'But he wrote us it was a boom town,' said Grace. 'What happened?'

'No way to tell right now,' grunted the halfbreed. 'The best we can do is fetch some clean bedding. You want to do that?'

Grace nodded and hurried through the door. Azul lifted Hope clear of the filthy bed and set her on the floor. He ripped the covers from the mattress and turned the thing over. Bugs ran quickly from the light, and when he slapped his hand against the palliasse, more dark shapes jetted from the sides and top.

'My God!' Grace Walls came in through the door, a bundle of fresh bedding clutched in her arms. 'Momma can't stay here.'

'Only place there is,' said Azul. 'Be more comfortable than the wagon.'

Grace stared at him, then said: 'Yes. You're right. I'll get the bed made up.'

Azul waited until she was finished, then lifted Hope on to the clean sheets. Grace settled the top covers over her mother and stared at the halfbreed.

'What are we going to do?'

Azul shrugged. 'I done what I promised. I brought you both through to Jericho, so now it's up to you.'

'You can't leave us here.' Grace's face got screwed up into tearful lines. 'That'd be like killing us.'

'I'll stay long enough to bury your mother,' Azul replied. 'Until then. No longer.'

'You're a hard bastard,' Grace snarled. 'A real bastard.'

All the old animosity returned: once again they were enemies trapped by a joint purpose.

'I done what I was paid for,' rasped Azul. 'Done it even when you lied to me. You can't ask much more than that. I'll hold on until your mother dies, then I quit.'

The door opened as Grace began to speak, and Joshua

tuck his lanky frame into the room. 'I got food ready. Best n the house. And on the house, seeing as how you're all my in.'

His adam's apple jerked up and down as he laughed, ouncing the thin strands of tie in obscene parody of umour. They followed him out.

The meal was served in the dining room attached to the otel. The room was heavy with dust, though every table was et in preparation. Knives and forks and spoons were laid ut alongside plates in which beetles scurried. There were roppings on the tablecloths, and the fringes were chewed y rats. The meal consisted of beans and bread, with a jug f coffee and a bottle of whisky to wash it down.

'I apologise for the poor fare,' said Joshua. 'But supplies ave been halted somewhat by the Indians. Indeed, many of ny people decided to move away after the recent troubles.'

'What troubles?' Azúl spooned beans into his mouth. 'We eard the Sioux were grouping on the Black Hills, but none topped us coming here.'

'They are all around.' Joshua poured coffee for Grace and hisky for himself and Azul. 'They watch me all the time. They raided my town a while ago, killing many of the towns-olk. The more cowardly element moved away, but I stayed n.'

'How many stayed with you, Uncle Josh?' Grace brushed ust from her skirt. 'We've not seen anyone else.'

'Nor shall you!' Joshua swallowed whisky and laughed. For they are all gone! All of the cowardly swine. All the pportunists who thought to cash in on my success. They ed after the last attack.'

'The last?' Azul set his glass down on the table, lifting a loud of dust from the cloth. 'How many you had?'

Joshua scratched his ear. 'I don't remember exactly. Six or even, I think. Abel left after one, because I sent him to Fort etterman to post a letter south. Thank God it arrived afely.'

'Abel?' grunted Azul. 'Who's Abel?'

'My cousin,' said Grace. 'Uncle Josh's son.'

'Yes.' Joshua raised his glass. 'My noble son who rode through the massed ranks of the hostile savages to take word south to my beloved relatives. Drinks are on the house, my friends. Lift your glasses in toast to my son, Abel.'

He stood up, swirling his arm about so that whisky slopped over the brim of the dirty glass.

'Where is he?' asked Azul.

Grace shrugged: 'I don't know.'

Joshua finished his toasting and sat down. 'You brought the . . . goods? You and my dear sister?'

'Yes, Uncle Josh,' said Grace. 'In the wagon.'

'Excellent.' The stringy-limbed man rubbed his hands together. 'Now that I have that silver I can begin to rebuild Jericho. People will flock from miles around.'

'Sure they will,' said Azul. 'But right now we'd best take a look at your sister.'

'Of course.' Joshua stood up. 'Dear Hope. Where is she? You said something about her being hurt, I recall.'

'Yeah.' Azul climbed to his feet. 'Bad hurt.'

'What happened?' Joshua led the way out of the dining room. 'Did the hostile savages attack you? I hope not. It does not pay a woman well to fall into their hands. Not at all. They are like madmen. There is no knowing the limits to which they go.'

'Why not clear the restaurant?' said Grace. 'Azul and I can look after momma.'

'Yes. Why not.' Joshua ducked his snow-white head. 'An excellent notion. I shall clear the restaurant and then prepare rooms for you both. Fortunately we are not booked as heavily as usual. You are lucky: in a few weeks this hotel would be occupied from ground to roof. Mmh! Yes, very lucky.'

He wandered away, beginning to pick up the plates and carry them through to the back of the restaurant as Grace and Azul walked back to Hope's room.

Grace was weeping silently, the tears coursing down her face so that what little make-up she had applied got smudged and ran in dark lines over her cheeks. Her shoulders trembled, and she clutched both arms across her breasts. Azul touched her shoulder.

'Don't worry. I'll get you out of here.'

The woman shook his touch away. 'I don't need no goddamn man to help me out!' Suddenly her voice was harsh, filled up with pain and fury. 'I got enough help from men already. It was a man got me in trouble the first time. That bastard turned his back and rode away. I learned my lesson then, and I never looked back.'

Azul paused, surprised by the vehemence of her voice, by the raw anger in it.

'Bastard got me pregnant,' snarled Grace. 'Left me with a kid I couldn't look after. A little girl. She died, so she missed out on the troubles a woman gets. She was only six months old. You know what I done then?'

Azul shook his head.

'I spent some time with momma,' said Grace, 'an' then I earned my own living. I'm not bad looking, so I reckoned the best way was to make men pay for their pleasures. How old do you think I am? I'll tell you – I'm thirty-five. I got work in a Dallas whorehouse, then I worked the river boats a few years. I saved my money and bought a place in Galenas. Best goddamn whoreshop you ever seen! I owned it and I ran it. I had the best girls and a touch of class. Men came from all over to bed my girls.

'Then momma sent me word she was in trouble. Poppa was dead and there was trouble at the mine. So I sold up. I put all my money into momma's holdings and we fixed for everything to be converted to silver. Momma had word from Uncle Josh about how well his town was doing, an' why didn't we come join him, so we headed north. Momma was going to run the hotel, and I was going to set up a new cat-house. It was a real good idea.

'Until now. Oh, sweet Jesus Christ! Why'd I ever do it?'

She turned and began pounding her fists against Azul's chest.

'Men are bastards,' she said over and over again. 'All of them. Just bastards.'

Azul grabbed her wrists and dragged her hands down.

'Not all,' he said. 'There's good and bad in everyone. You just got a rotten deal.'

Grace collapsed against him. 'Why me?'

'I don't know,' said the halfbreed. 'Why anyone?'

He folded his arms around her and waited until the weeping was stopped. Then he stood her upright again and said, 'Let's check your mother.'

Grace nodded, producing a lace handkerchief to blot her tears. 'I'm sorry. Please forgive me.'

'Nothing to forgive,' said Azul. 'There's nothing wrong with weeping.'

'You don't cry,' said Grace. 'You just keep pushing on.'

'I've shed tears.' Azul smiled without showing any humour. 'For people I loved.'

He pushed the woman before him, turning her towards the door of her mother's room. Grace looked back once, smiling, then opened the door.

Hope Walls was rigid on the bed. Her hands were thrust out to clutch the sheets and her broken legs were dragged up against her stomach so that the covers bulked loosely over her body. Her face was set in a smile, the mouth drawn back under the hollow sockets of her eyes. The sheets were stained with blood where she had torn the splints and bandages away, and the open wounds on her legs stank of putrescent flesh.

Grace screamed.

Azul crossed to the table where a note was lodged under the water pot.

It read: *Thank you for bringing me home. I want to die here. So use what I brought to start again. Joshua will look after you. Don't forget to pay Azul. We owe him $1000.*

It was signed: *Your loving mother, Hope.*

Grace went on screaming until Azul slapped her face. All her toughness evaporated under the onslaught of this second shock, and she collapsed to her knees beside the bed. Her body shook as silent tears coursed afresh down her cheeks and her lips moved slowly, forming indistinct words. Azul waited, trying to make out what she was saying.

Gradually, like the rolling thunder of a distant storm, the words became clear.

'Bastards. All of them. Bastards.'

She repeated it over and over again until Azul took hold of her shoulders and lifted her upright. She made no protest, merely remaining stiff beneath his touch. Then she squared her shoulders and turned to face him.

'Uncle Josh lied to us.' Her voice was flat, drained of emotion. 'He told us this was a boom town. He wrote us that if we brought the silver and the deeds up here, we'd have a new home. A new start. He said we could stay here the rest of our lives.'

'Your mother did,' murmured Azul. 'And your uncle's crazy. Now let's see about burying Hope.'

Grace nodded. 'Yes, that's what she wanted.'

The hardware store was boarded up, but rain and snow had rotted the planks so that they came loose easily. Inside, Azul found picks and shovels and a few plain coffins stacked against the rear wall. He dragged his loot over to the hotel and went to find Joshua.

The crazy old man was in the kitchen, dutifully scrubbing the used plates and setting them carefully in a filthy cupboard.

'May I help you, sir?' He seemed not to recognise Azul. 'I fear we are a trifle short-staffed at present.'

'You got a cemetery?' asked the halfbreed.

'Why yes.' Joshua dried his hands on a strip of mouse-nibbled towel. 'Has there been an accident?'

'Your sister died.' Azul spoke slowly, his Apache upbringing instilling a sense of reverence for the insane. 'We have to bury her.'

'Hope?' Joshua blinked. 'But Hope is in Mexico.'

'Hope's gone,' said Azul. 'Where's the cemetery?'

'Just west of town.' Joshua was confused now. 'Beyond the stream.'

'Thanks.' Azul turned away.

'My pleasure, sir.' Joshua went back to the sink. 'Should you require anything else, please let me know.'

He began to hum softly, his sister – and everything else – forgotten behind the haze of his madness. Whatever world he now inhabited, it did not allow for any recognition of real events. Azul left him to his dreams and returned to the bedroom.

Grace had washed her mother and straightened the thin limbs. Hope Walls was once more dressed in her black widow's weeds, her hands crossed on her breast and that same calm smile on her face.

'I can't close her eyes,' said Grace dully. 'You can't bury someone with open eyes.'

Azul slid the lids down and weighted them with dimes. As he bent over the corpse he caught a scent of the rotted flesh. 'I got a coffin outside,' he said. 'Let's bury her.'

They wrapped Hope in the sheet and Azul carried the frail body out to the porch. He set her down in the plain pine box and used the shovel to hammer the lid in place. Then he loaded the coffin inside the wagon that had brought Hope to her last resting place and steered the mules back across the bridge.

On the far side of the stream a trail led off to the west. A mile farther on there was a split in the ridge that opened on to a broad meadow. A wooden fence blocked entrance, a sign hung above the creosoted gate announcing the place as The Jericho Garden of Rest. The grass was dotted with crosses and headstones.

Azul halted the wagon and carried the coffin inside the graveyard. Then he took the pick and the shovel and dug a trench, six by six by two. The afternoon was fading into evening before he finished, and as he stamped the soil down over the coffin the discordant notes of a bugle rang along the valley.

'What's that?' Grace started. 'Is it the Army?'

Azul peered back through the growing dusk. 'No. Your uncle's sounding the *Last Post*.'

'Crazy bastard.' Grace's voice was empty of emotion. 'Poor, mad old man.'

'Yeah.' Azul stamped the last divot in place. 'He's blowing his trumpet in Jericho. An' he sure brought the Walls down.'

Chapter Thirteen

Full darkness settled over Jericho as they returned from the graveyard. Lights shone from the frontage of the hotel, but the other buildings remained blank and silent. The tinny notes of a nickelodeon rattled strident sound in echoes across the bleak frontages.

Azul got the livery stable opened up and found sufficient hay to bed and feed the mules and the grey stallion for the night. Then he escorted Grace back to the hotel.

Joshua was waiting for them as they entered the Jericho Palace.

'I have your rooms ready,' he said. 'And dinner will be served in thirty minutes.'

The rooms were on the upper level. The curtains covering the windows were grey with dust and the carpets were gnawed by mice. The sheets on the beds were grey and fouled by droppings. Grace said, 'I can't sleep here.'

Azul said, 'It's here or the wagon. Which do you want?'

'Hell!' The woman pounded the filthy blankets, provoking an exit of insects. 'Here, I guess.'

They went back to the wagon and fetched clean linen to their rooms. Re-made the beds and then went down to the dining-room, where Joshua was busy laying out plates.

'My friends,' he said. 'I have prepared a special meal. What a pity that poor Hope cannot join us. Still, I have set a small collation aside for her. I shall serve you and then her.'

Azul and Grace sat down at the only clean table. Joshua brought them soup. A drowned weevil floated in Grace's bowl.

'I'm not very hungry,' she said. 'What's the next course?'

'Forgive me.' Joshua bowed low and removed both bowls. 'There are problems with the staff. The next course is steak. Prepared by my own hands.'

The steaks were thick with fungus, giving off a sickly sweet odour of rotten meat. They came with potatoes and greens; both vegetables were old and diseased.

'Please forgive me if I don't join you,' said Joshua. 'I must see to my sister.'

He left the dining room, and Azul shoved his mouldering plate aside.

'Go get some food from the wagon,' he said. 'I'll see what he's doing.'

Grace nodded and quit the room. Azul followed Joshua down the corridor.

The lanky man paced through the dust covering the moth-eaten carpets. He checked each room along the way until he came to the room he had given to Hope. Then he screamed, backing out with hands clutched about his face.

'She's gone! She's gone!' He staggered back against the far side of the corridor. 'She's not there.'

He hit the wall and slid down in a cloud of dust. His hands scrabbled over his face, the nails ripping bloody tracks down his cheeks, the points ending at his lower lips, where they tucked into the membranes and began to spill blood down his chin.

'She's dead,' Azul said. 'She was buried today.'

'Flies! They'll eat her,' mumbled Joshua. 'As flies to wanton boys are we to the gods: they kill us for their sport! The gods are just, and of our pleasant vices make instruments to plague us.'

Azul hit him once. Hard, in the face.

Joshua's head slumped back and his body got loose. Azul lowered him to the floor.

Grace came back with a sack bundled up in her arms.

'What are you doing?' she cried.

Azul turned: 'Your uncle's gone over,' he said. 'He's mad as a hare in March. Like he ate loco weed.'

'Oh Jesus Christ!' Grace dropped the bundle of food she was carrying. 'What do we do now?'

'Carry on,' said Azul, picking up the supplies. 'That's all we can do.'

'I'll take your word.' Grace nodded, reaching down to collect her dropped bundle. 'Whatever you say.'

They hauled Joshua to his room and got him settled on the bed. Grace cleaned his face and they left him snoring resonantly. In the bar below, the nickelodeon ground to a stop and tomb-like quiet descended over the ghost town. Azul saw Grace to her room and passed her one of the Winchesters.

'Best lock your door,' he suggested. 'Might be safest.'

'Uncle Josh wouldn't harm me,' Grace murmured. 'I don't think he's dangerous.'

'It's not him I'm thinking of,' the halfbreed replied. 'There's been someone out to stop you all the way from New Mexico. No reason why he won't try again.'

Grace gasped, suddenly remembering the attacks. 'My God! I'd forgotten.' She frowned. 'Who is it, though?'

'Your cousin's not around,' Azul grunted. 'And he was the one took the letter to the fort.'

'Abel?' Grace shook her head. 'I've not seen him in ten years.'

'But he knew where your mother was,' said Azul. 'And if he read the letter, he'd have known about the silver.'

'Abel can't be more than twenty,' argued the woman. 'And he was a timid little boy.'

Azul shrugged. 'Greed can change a man. Lock your door and keep the Winchester close by. If anything happens, yell.'

Grace nodded and stepped inside the room. Azul waited until the door closed and the bolts on the far side slid shut, then he went into his own quarters.

He glanced around: the room was furnished with a single bed, a wash-stand, a chair and a small cupboard. A window looked on to the street with a narrow balcony running the length of the frontage. The halfbreed set the lamp he was carrying down on the wash-stand and checked his guns. Then he shoved the pillows down under the sheets so that the bed got bulked up as if a body occupied the centre. He shrugged into his topcoat and eased the window open, climbing out on to the balcony. He slid the window gently shut and crouched behind the cover of the balustrade.

The night was chilly, the sky clear, with the stars shining like pinpricks of light gleaming through a blue velvet blanket. Azul's moccasins padded silently over the woodwork as he cat-footed to the far end of the platform and swung his legs over the retaining wall. He climbed on to the porch and dropped to the street below.

A light was still shining from the front of the hotel and the door was open. He eased inside after checking the street and moved silently to the rear of the building. There was a door opening into the kitchen: Azul slid the bolts home. Then he moved stealthily through the rooms, checking the windows. All were shut tight.

When he was satisfied that the only way into the Jericho Palace was through the open front door, he entered the small office behind the reception desk and settled on the chair there.

With his rifle cradled in his arms, he sat watching the narrow crack between door and frame.

The moon was waning, shedding just enough light to illumine the street between the pools of shadow, and the lantern burning on the desk outside lit the vestibule. An owl hooted. Somewhere in the hills a cougar screamed, the rasping cry echoing through the empty town. Rodents scrambled on the boardwalk, emitting shrill squeals as they argued over scraps of discarded food. In the quiet, Azul could hear the rats gnawing at the food in the kitchen.

Then he caught the sound he was expecting.

From the far end of mainstreet there came the slow *clop* of cautious hoofs. The halfbreed lifted to his feet, ears straining to catch the dull thudding. His Apache-trained hearing identified the riders within seconds: three horses.

Iron-shod and therefore belonging to white men. Moving at a walking pace: quietly. As if the riders were anxious to avoid detection.

The sounds got louder as the horses approached the hotel. Then ceased. Azul heard the door of the stable creak as it opened; a muttered conversation. The double *snap* of a carbine's action. Azul flattened against the wall of the office, hiding himself behind the door.

Boot heels drummed on the sidewalk, scattering the quarrelsome mice. And the main door eased slowly inwards.

A harsh voice whispered, 'Keep it quiet. This is the only place they'll be. Ain't nowhere else fit to live in.'

Three men came inside.

Azul watched them through the crack of the office door.

The leader was a young man, wispy brown hair hanging to his shoulders from beneath a silver-banded black stetson. He wore a loden coat over black pants tucked inside worn black boots. The ivory grip of a Smith & Wesson Schofield shone pale from above a black leather holster. He shucked clear of his coat, transferring the Winchester he carried from hand to hand as the coat fell to the floor. A black vest and a white shirt covered his chest, and his thin-lipped mouth was set in a contemptuous smile.

The other two wore dark stormcoats that they eased down with practised skill. One was about thirty a stubbly beard covering his lower jaw and a dark brown stetson shading pale green eyes, the left pulled out of line by a knife-scar that ran from temple to chin. He held a Browning shotgun, both hammers cocked, and a brace of Remington's Army model revolvers holstered butts-forward on his hips.

The last man was around twenty-five, his face clean-shaven beneath a coonskin cap. He wore a shirt of fringed leather and a pair of broadcloth trousers. A wide belt spanned his swollen waist, supporting a sheath that contained a Bowie knife and an empty holster. The pistol was clutched in his right hand: a Colt's Cavalry model. The hammer was full cocked and the trigger drawn back to maximum tension by the chewed forefinger.

The leader halted, lifting a finger to his narrow mouth as he pointed the Winchester at the office.

'He sleeps in there some nights,' he whispered. 'Go check it.'

The man in the coonskin cap moved towards the door. Like Azul, he wore moccasins, but decorated with coloured beads and pieces of quill that had been dyed to form patterns of scarlet and blue down the sides. He peered in through the door, shoving it back against the wall.

Azul sank to the floor, holding his Winchester ready to fire.

'Ain't nobody here,' murmured the intruder. 'Reckon they must be asleep.'

'Upstairs, then.' The brown-haired man had a slight lisp, so that it sounded like *Upthtairth. Leth go.*

Azul went on watching through the crack until he heard their feet moving along the upper corridor. Then he eased clear of the office and went up behind them. All his Apache caution came into play as he stalked the three men. His feet made no sound on the worn carpet covering the stairs, and a certain element of Apache humour entered the situation.

Grace Walls had tricked him for as long as she could. Had fooled him and lied to him; now she would get a surprise due her as a result of her deception. He chose to leave it that long before he killed the three intruders and thus fulfilled his original promise. But first, Grace could worry a bit.

He halted at the head of the stairs, crouching down as the black-vested man tapped on her door.

'What?' Her voice was thick with sleep. 'Who is it?'

'Abel, cousin. Let me in.'

'Abel?' The halfbreed heard her climb out of bed. 'Hold on.' Then: 'Azul? Azul! Where are you?'

Abel lifted his foot and kicked the door. The timbers, eaten by woodworm, gave easily. The door sprang open.

Grace screamed, the sound cut off abruptly as the stock of

the Winchester slammed against her jaw.

Abel snarled, 'The guide must be in the other room. Kill him!'

The Colt blasted the lock apart and the door tore clear of the hinges as both hired guns slammed their shoulders against the wood. The Browning roared twice. Then a nasal voice shouted: 'He ain't here! Bastard's fooled us!'

'Goddamn it!' snarled Abel. 'Where is he?'

His tone got softer. Azul went on waiting.

'Grace?' There was the sound of a hand slapping against a cheek. 'Where is he?'

'I don't know.'

'Cousin, you gotta know. You hired him, now tell me where he is.'

'I don't know. I swear I don't.'

'An' I'll bet you don't know where the silver is, either.'

The same hollow sound of open palm striking flesh echoed down the corridor. Joshua Walls opened his door and stumbled out.

'Abel! Abel, my son. Did the heathen savages delay you?'

'You goddamn crazy bastard!'

The corridor got lit up by the flaring muzzle of the Winchester. Joshua stumbled back, his jacket darkened by the outpouring of blood from the three bullets that struck his lanky body. The hired guns fired on pure instinct. The Colt and both Remingtons adding to the destruction of the crazy old man. Bullets struck his face and chest, adding momentum to his fall so that his feet left the threadbare carpet and he flew through the air to crash down no more than four feet from Azul's position.

'Leave him!' Abel shouted. 'That goddamn old fool kept me runnin' his stinkin' ghost town too long. Leave him for the rats. That's all he deserves.'

'Where's that guide, though?' asked the man in the coon-skin cap. 'His horse is in the stable, so he's around some-where.'

'Where's the silver?' snarled the scar-faced man. 'That's what we come for.'

'Yes,' said Abel. 'Where is it, Grace?'

'Go to hell!'

Another slap echoed along the corridor. Azul stood up.

'You'll have to tell me.' Abel's voice was softly evil. 'I can make you. I can, Grace. Believe me. Look. It's amazing, Grace.'

Chapter Fourteen

Azul moved forwards, his steps hidden by Grace's screams.

He reached the door as the scar-faced man began to thumb fresh loads into the shotgun. The man in the coonskin cap was ejecting the spent shells from his Colt and giggling as Abel bent over the woman.

Grace Walls's nightdress was on the floor, torn in two. Abel's Winchester lay on top of the ripped silk. His hands were fumbling over the buttons of his pants and his legs were spread wide, forcing Grace's apart.

'Hope we all get a turn,' chuckled the leather-shirted gunslinger. 'Looks like real tasty meat down there.'

'You just shot your last load,' snarled Azul. And squeezed the trigger of the carbine.

The leather shirt exploded inwards as the ·44-40 calibre slug ripped through the material. The coonskin cap flew loose from the man's head as he pitched forwards across the bed. The bullet tore in through his back, puncturing the left lung and then deflecting off the forward ribs before emerging in a huge gout of crimson that splattered over Abel's naked buttocks and the woman's stomach.

Azul levered and fired again as the man with the scattergun swung round, dragging the right-hand hammer back.

He was fast.

Very fast: he triggered as he turned, spreading a swathe of buckshot towards the door.

Azul dropped to his knees, letting the discharge of the shotgun pass over his head. But the movement shifted his own aim so that the Winchester's bullet glanced off the scar-faced man's scapula, tearing a raw, red gouge across his shirt and throwing his arms up to expend the second barrel of the Browning into the ceiling.

Grace screamed again.

The scar-faced man cursed and dropped the shotgun, reaching for the two Remingtons.

Azul triggered a third shot.

It went in just above the belt, turning the man over in a jack-knife dive that slammed his head against the floor. It pierced his belly and came out above the pelvic girdle in a foul-smelling column of blood and pulverised kidney. The halfbreed worked the action again, his fourth bullet blasting through the dome of scar-face's skull so that the entire cranium imploded. The man's hat flew loose from his head, expelled by the fragmentation of bone and blood and brain matter that fluttered his thinning hair in a wavering circle about the central hole. The bullet tore down through the soft membranes of the brain to rip clear from the lower jaw. Great gouts of blood spurted from the entry hole, the nostrils, the mouth, and the ragged gap beneath the chin.

Abel Walls lurched through the window clutching his opened pants in one hand and the Smith & Wesson in the other.

'Get him!' Grace shrieked. 'Kill the bastard! Kill him!'

Azul ducked back as a shot blasted into the room. Grace began to scream again. Boots pounded along the balcony.

Azul ran down the corridor, launching himself down the stairs in a headlong run. He shouldered through the front door and angled the rifle towards the darting shape up the street.

He fired twice.

The first shot, snapped off as scudding cloud covered the moon, missed. The second pitched the running figure forwards.

The Smith & Wesson barked again, the bullet sharding splinters of rotten wood from the supporting pole to Azul's right. Then Abel disappeared into the alleyway leading to the stable.

Azul levered the Winchester and ran through the shadows covering the sidewalk.

He reached the alley and blasted three random shots into the darkness. The only answer was the dull *thump* of his bullets hitting the swinging door of the stable. He paced along the narrow street with the rifle canted over his flat stomach. Got to the entrance.

And shouted: 'Abel! Throw your gun down an' come out!'

Then he hammered the stock of the Winchester against the door and ran round to the back as Abel ploughed ·44 slugs through the wood.

He reached the back and dropped the rifle to the ground, hauling his Colt clear of the holster as he powered in through the rear entrance.

Abel was crouched down inside the first stall. He had the Smith & Wesson angled at the main doors, his wrist braced against the wooden partition. The stable was around one hundred and fifty feet long, and the mules and Azul's stallion were bedded to either side. The halfbreed let his rush carry him down to the floor, wary of harming the animals.

Abel Walls had no such inhibitions. He loosed off six rounds of rapid fire and then began to climb the ladder leading to the loft. Azul flattened against the straw, conscious of moisture beneath his belly, and the hurried scuttling of small animals that fled in terror of the flames and thunder filling the barn.

He fired twice, watching his bullets dance splinters off the ladder a foot below Abel's heels. Then he lifted his aim and emptied the Colt so that the ladder fell apart, trapping Abel in the loft.

The brown-haired killer laughed. 'What you gonna do now?'

He snapped the Smith & Wesson open, relying on the instant discharge of the spent cartridges to gain him the advantage over the slower loading Colt. He started to thumb fresh loads into the chambers, standing up on the edge of the loft as he jeered at the halfbreed.

Azul holstered the Colt and stepped out to the centre of the aisle. He reached down to pluck the throwing knife clear of his moccasin. Then swung his arm back and hurled the knife in a straight line that ended where Abel's throat connected with his jaw.

The slender blade penetrated the soft flesh of the chin's underside. It drove on to pin the tongue against the roof of the mouth and drive its tip upwards through the nasal membranes. Abel choked and dropped his gun. His hands reached up to clutch at the leather-wrapped hilt protruding from his neck, then he gasped and folded forwards.

He fell clear of the loft, slamming against the ground below with sufficient force to drive the point of the knife through his neck-bones. He went on trying to drag the blade clear, his mouth jerking as he tried to speak. With his tongue pinned he could say nothing, so as he fought the pain only blood came out of his mouth.

Azul smiled without humour and dragged the knife away. The blade was red. And got redder when the halfbreed slashed it across the wound, opening Abel's throat like the belly of a gutted fish.

Azul stepped clear of the discharge, waiting until all the blood was pumped clear, then dragged the body out of the stable and dropped it in the alley behind. The rats came out as soon as he was gone, and began to eat.

Grace Walls was dressed and waiting when he returned to the Jericho Palace, clutching a carbine in her hands and looking both angry and grateful.

'What happened?' she asked. 'Is he dead?'

Azul nodded. 'Yeah. I killed him.'

'My own cousin.' She lowered the carbine. 'Who'd have thought it?'

'That's the trouble with blood relations,' rasped Azul.

'But at least Abel got caned.'

The next day they emptied the wagon of furniture on Grace's insistence and shifted it all inside the hotel. The dark-haired woman spent the next few days cleaning the bridal suite and the kitchen. Azul dragged the old furniture out and replaced it with the new: part of the Jericho Palace looked almost fresh. Azul buried Abel and the two gunmen at the far end of the cemetery and Joshua at the front, alongside the grave of his wife and next to the mound that marked Hope Walls's grave. He found two marble slabs in the hardware store, and spent three days chipping letters into the surface.

One read: '*Hope Walls. A brave lady who died fighting.*'

The other just said: '*Joshua Walls. Mayor of Jericho.*'

The graves occupied by Abel and the others were left unmarked.

When that task was finished Azul broke the wagon apart and stripped the silver clear of the planks. He used the smithy attached to the stable to melt the ore into usable ingots that he left to cool and then stacked in the office of the hotel. Grace gave him two of the blocks in lieu of ready cash: their value exceeded the second $500, but it was the only way she could pay him.

'Besides,' she said, 'you done a lot more than we asked, so I reckon you're owed it.'

'What are you going to do?' Azul enquired. 'You want me to take you south?'

Grace shook her head. 'I got a mule team that I know how to handle. There's a spare wagon in the stable. I think I'll stay on here. Maybe the people will come back. Or maybe new folks'll come in. Either way, I own the town now that Uncle Josh is dead. I never owned a town before.'

Azul shrugged. 'Up to you. I aim to leave in the morning.'

'Do as you like,' said Grace. 'I paid you, so we're all square.'

'Yeah.' Azul paused as a familiar sound intruded on his senses. 'There's riders coming.'

He picked up his rifle. Grace lifted hers.

From the southern ridge there came a line of horsemen. They were dressed in the blue shirts and yellow-stripped pants of the United States Cavalry. They came down the slope behind the lead riders. One man held a pennant aloft, the guidon fluttering in the morning breeze. To either side sat two disparate men, one chubby, with thick moustaches of dark hair curving across his cheeks; to the right rode a man dressed in a buckskin coat, with long blond hair falling from under a curly-brimmed cavalry hat that sported a feather on the left side. A wispy beard and fragile moustache blew about his narrow chin. He raised his hand to halt the column as it crossed the bridge.

Then he rode forwards.

'Ma'am.' He touched his hat in salute. 'Mister?'

'Gunn,' Azul replied. 'Matthew Gunn. The lady is Grace Walls. She owns the town.'

'Delighted to hear that.' The fair-haired man slapped a gloved hand against his thigh. 'I am Major George Armstrong Custer. Perhaps you've heard of me?'

Azul shook his head.

Custer pouted and stroked his moustache. 'You will soon, my friend. I am on my way to defeat the Sioux and the Cheyenne. The hostiles are gathering just north of here, at a place called the Little Bighorn. Maybe you've seen them?'

Again, Azul shook his head.

'No matter.' Custer brushed his beard. 'We shall clear the territory of savages. Perhaps you might care to join us.'

Azul shook his head again.

'I'm moving south. I got no quarrel with the Plains Indians.'

'I think I detect the tones of a halfbreed.' Custer sneered. 'Perhaps you steer clear of fighting your red brothers.'

'I only fight them when I need to,' rasped Azul. 'But not to clear them off land they own.'

'I could have you shot for that!' Custer snapped. 'All I need to do is give the signal.'

'You'd be dead first,' snarled the halfbreed. 'You lift your goddamn hand an' I'll put a bullet through your gut.'

Custer swallowed hard. 'That's strong talk, my friend. But still, I can't win all the battles. I'll let you go. We'll forget this happened.'

Azul turned away. Grace came running after him.

'You going now?'

The halfbreed nodded. 'Not much point in staying.'

'Take care,' she said. And planted a kiss on his mouth. 'Be careful.'

'You're going to stay?' asked Azul.

Grace smiled and pointed at the soldiers lined up along the street. 'There's customers waiting,' she said. 'I'd be stupid to turn down good business. I could start a going trade if these boys come back from that Bighorn place. Soldiers like to relax after a fight.'

Azul got up on his horse and rode away to the south.

And another Western series from Sphere:

GUNSLINGER

CHARLES C. GARRETT

In the West that Ryker knew, life was cheap. Only from death could a man like Ryker make a living – gunsmith turned gunslinger, he was the best killer around, a craftsman of his cruel trade.

GUNSLINGER 1: MASSACRE TRAIL 75p

GUNSLINGER 2: THE GOLDEN GUN 65p

GUNSLINGER 3: THE WHITE APACHE 75p

GUNSLINGER 4: 50 CALIBRE KILL 85p

GUNSLINGER 5: ARIZONA BLOODLINE 85p

GUNSLINGER 6: REBEL VENGEANCE 85p

GUNSLINGER 7: DEATH CANYON 85p